Do You Know Why You Can't Feel My Pain?

Do You Know Why You Can't Feel My Pain?

Overcoming the pain of separation

Lady Ola

Dedication

This book is dedicated to the memories of my father, Late Chief Ezekiel Ojutomori Ogundipe, for being the best dad that ever lived, and to my mother, late Mrs Ruth Oreoluwa Ogundipe, who taught me the way of the Lord. I also dedicate this work to my wonderful husband, Olusegun Victor Aigbogun, my sweetheart and best friend, who loved and believed in me when I didn't believe in myself.

I also dedicate this book to all of you who are drowning in the pool of betrayal, neglect, and separation from your desired place or person. This book is for you!

Appreciation

My utmost appreciation to God Almighty, through Jesus Christ, has given me the gift of salvation and grace to transform the storm of life into an experience of strength, from where I have drawn the inspiration behind this book.

A big thank you to my best friend and husband for being my mentor and my Pastor, who has worked tirelessly with me day in, day out to make this book a success. I wouldn't have been able to write this book if God had not provided my husband to support me and pull me through.

To my darling children, Michelle, Samuel, Kevin, Gabriel and Jeremiah for their support and faith in me. Thank you guys, for your contributions. My big sister, Mofoluke Ogundipe Sloan, who did not stop pestering me about writing this book, and to my siblings, Tosin Taiwo, Yemi Ogundipe, Lanre Ogundipe and Mojisola Ogunkanmi, who stood by me through thick and thin during my life's ordeals.

To my Spiritual Father, Bishop Joby Brady, the man of God, who spoke the word of prophecy regarding the creation of this book.

Finally, my appreciation goes to the entire Congregation of Grace Outreach Riyadh Church, for providing the platform to fulfil my God given destiny.

Foreword

I met Pastor Victor and Ola in Riyadh Saudi Arabia through a mutual acquaintance. Not having been to that nation before, I felt a bit of trepidation at the invitation of ministering there. The political and religious climate in Riyadh is ever changing and the fact that they were able to build a wonderful ministry there is unprecedented. However, at their request and God's release I made my way there. I've been in Ministry for over 40 years. I have literally seen it and heard it all. Nevertheless, Pastor Ola Aigbogun's story is one in which I immediately became captivated by. To meet her is to see grace and humility personified. She walks next to her husband in strength and dignity in a way that reminds me of my wife. You will not see the success of Dr. Victor Aigbogun and Grace Outreach Church and not attribute it to their ability to lead with structure, order and oversight together. They are so submissive, kind-hearted and respectful in every area. Together they emulate the concept that to be successful and/ or go to the next level you have to make strategic connections to greatness. I stress the word together because Pastor Ola's account, which you will read in the next few pages, is a remarkable story of the pain of separation and finding God in the middle of it. How do you manage departure from loved ones? How do you manage the seemingly death of dreams and desires? How do you manage pain in any form? Pastor Ola demonstrates, through her transparency, the transitions through her painful times, and her triumph over it all. I believe, in this season, that you will be challenged by this timely and timeless read. Turn every page with expectation that God will turn your life toward the direction of destiny.

Bishop Joby R. Brady
Potters House of North Dallas
The Presiding Prelate, River Fellowship Intl.

From the Desk of Pastor Victor…

Mopelola is my wife. She is the woman who changed my life, and my world. It took a while for me to discover the secret of her power; the power to give me the 360 degree turnaround I needed to transform from being the man I was, to the man God intended me to be. Her secret is well revealed in this book. It is life. Life defined her character, and her experiences changed her as a person, making her the best companion in my divine assignment.

Life's experiences are acquired through the spheres of our encounters, and our exposure to the troubled waters of life.

It has never been so obvious that, the most subtle pain that eats us up and forms the bedrock of our responses, crises and rifts in life, is the pain of separation from relationships.

Until you read this book, you will never understand why we are cut so deeply when betrayed and denied by friends and family. You will never understand why you need to free yourself from the guilt you are facing when in situations beyond your control, where it seems like you yourself betrayed your friends or family.

The way Pastor Ola had used her personal life story, synergised with biblical stories, especially the expression of the pain of Jesus at Gethsemane, to presents answers to relationship crises and the pain it brings, is far beyond words.

Those who are battling with the guilt of failure in relationships will find this book a source of relief. It will help build the motivation required to move past their guilt. Most importantly, this book will be a great source of counsel to those who are still grieving the loss of a person, place or purpose. Being divorced from your investment is a painful ordeal; it takes time to heal. This book is such a great spirit lifting, mind freeing and hope building resource for anyone experiencing the pain of separation.

Dr. Victor O. Aigbogun
The President & Oversight Apostle
Grace Outreach Riyadh Apostolicity

Introduction

*For I know the thoughts that I think toward you, says
the LORD, thoughts of peace and not of evil, to give
you a future and a hope. (Jeremiah 29:11 NKJV)*

Life is a teacher; life is a mentor; life molds; and
life builds. It all stems from our experiences and
exposures. Our expectations rarely materialise, yet
things we least expect, more often than not, end up
at our bosoms. The truth lies in the grace of God —
it gives us the privilege to gain the experiences we
need. My own experiences in life have never been
anything short of the proof of what life can offer, and
what God can do.

I have often asked the question ... why me?
On other occasions, I have forgotten to ask ... why
me? In my darkest moments, through my hardest
times, and on the days I think are my worst, I asked
God," **Why Me?**" I reflect back on what I've been
through, focusing on every detail, and think about

what God put me through. During each of those difficult moments, I would have asked the question: **WHY ME?**

However, when I look back on the times between my troubles and pleasure, I realised that, in those moments of sunlight and joy, I never asked God the question: **WHY ME?**

There are many people in the world who face trials and tribulations, torments and failures. The truth, though, is that these experiences in life prepare us for when that great things happen.

So, I thought I would write this book, by the power of the Holy Spirit, to express how important it is to not take one side of the story and draw conclusions about yourself; likewise, don't view the other side of the story and draw conclusions on others. The journey of life can easily make you judge people, and vice versa. You will become a victor when you have mastered the ability to see both sides of the story. It will help you understand why people will not follow you, why people will leave you, abandon you or reject you at a time you least expect them to, and why the people you never anticipated in your life, show up and support you when you least expected them to. The balance of this empowers you with the knowledge that people cannot feel your pain.

Emotional pain is the experience of agony that is often expressed internally, but manifests itself externally. It is the pain deep within our hearts that is triggered by the actions of others, or by our own error in perception or judgment. The realisation of what has been done to you, and its implications, can eventually lead to long term agony within your heart. Those who inflicted this heart breaking pain on you will never know or feel your pain. They won't know as they've never experienced what you're experiencing. Often, these hurtful people will take great pleasure from their actions, with no understanding of the devastation they have caused you, and how much of your life they have drained. They will never know your pain. No wonder it is considered your pain; it is your pain and you must know how to deal with it.

The capacity of Humankind was not obvious at the beginning. Nor was the reasoning behind God's creation of Man (human beings) fully revealed. The foundation of what Man can do, and what Man has become, is now better known. However, what Man really is, was only revealed with time … when Adam was created. He was situated in a place of joy, a place of grace, a place of abundance. What he could become was expressed to him in the form of blessings and commands. God said to Adam, "be fruitful" (Gen.1:22), which effectively meant that God had given Adam the power to be fruitful. Until God had uttered this command and blessing, Adam was powerless to do this. "Have dominion," God said. Likewise, Adam didn't possess dominion until God offered it, thereby releasing this power to him. The journey of creation is part of life's experience. When the occasion to exert dominion arose, the creature he was supposed to have dominion over, took this power from Adam, leaving him unable to apply it. Adam's response to Satan initiated the exposition of Man.

Setting yourself free from the pain of separation will help you realise the magnitude of your potential. Separation can be painful and bloody. It is a culmination of the pain of rejection, disloyalty and lack of commitment.

When something dear to you, something you've dedicated your life to and believed to be forever, is taken away, it can be emotionally damaging.

But I want you to know that nothing reveals the power of your potential better than the pain of separation. Losing a job you loved can open the door to better opportunities. Separation from whatever, whoever and wherever often helps prepare you for better and greater prospects.

What I hope to achieve is for you to have the ability to stand above the pain. No one will ever truly feel your pain. Without the ability to feel your pain, it will be impossible for them to recognise your power.

Mother Teresa once said, ***"The most terrible poverty is loneliness and the feeling of being unloved"***. Another one of my favourite quotes is by Bess Myerson, ***"To fall in love is awfully simple, but to fall out of love is simply awful"***. When separation takes place, either from someone or something, the key drivers of our emotions originate from feeling unloved, a projection of loneliness and the countenance of poverty. It throws us into the pool of agony, ballooned by our sense of rejection, ultimately drowning us in a pool of misery.

Every ounce of your dream could be shattered if you are crushed by the pain of separation. It is down to you to prevent this because your dream is not part of a one-stage process. To arrive at your destination often requires taking different steps and stops. Think about it — it applies to those of us who believe in the biblical truth of creation, and even to those who don't believe it as the truth but just regard it as a story, the story of God and Adam. It must have been awfully overwhelming for God to let go of Adam, both physically and spiritually. Despite the intricacies of the story being spiritually complicated, if the separation never occurred, based on the literary expression of the story, Adam would not have known how strong he was and how powerful his seed would become. God knew Adam would move onto a new phase of life, becoming the man who possessed the power of dominion, the power to subdue and multiply, but the separation was not easy. That is why I know that, whatever you might be going through, you cannot let separation and its pain hold you back. The pain of separation empowers you to prepare for greater things. You will never know what you are capable of doing until you experience the kind of pain that enables you to reveal your power and dominion.

This is a season for you to discover your new strength. You can easily make destiny stand still if you don't know how to manage the pain of separation. Life is always beautiful, with new beginnings.

CHAPTERS OF THE BOOK

Chapter One

Things You Weren't Told Growing Up

He replied to him, "Who is my mother, and who are my brothers?" Pointing to his disciples, he said, "Here are my mother and my brothers ..."
Matthew 12:48-49

It has never ceased to amaze me how siblings, children of the same parents, born of the same father and mother, end up as the worst of enemies in adulthood. Even between mothers and daughters, fathers and sons, as adults, I see deep-rooted pain and anger expressed in indescribable acrimonies. In the few years that I was privileged to Pastor and counsel women from different walks of lives, I noticed and dealt with a prevalence of relationship issues that originated from unresolved conflicts amongst siblings. It is obvious, despite how obvious it may seem, but we easily forget that 20 children cannot live together for 20 years. That is one thing we were never explicitly told. Our parents may have never informed us that five children, who grew up in the same household, would someday be separated. We grew up with the belief that, contrary to the obvious, we would stay together forever. Subsequently, as we grow up, the subtle process of separation begins. Separation will always be associated with pain; a pain that gradually, but psychologically, manifests itself in our actions towards others, driven by our expectations.

My brother believed he could call me, at any time, with requests for help. He lacked consciousness of the fact that this could not continue forever. The joy and the love, the good times we had growing up, are things that did not prepare us for reality, that this phase would pass, that we would all individually progress into a different and new phase of life. A phase where my brother would no longer be the most important person in my life; and equally, I no longer important to him. Different to how it was growing up. This is the root cause of crises that arise amongst families that were once 'tight'.

A lady once came to me in tears. She displayed such a sorrowful disposition at the altar, unable to control her tears, that I asked her to book an appointment to see me. When she finally came to see me in my office, I was amazed at how much anger she harboured in her heart towards her own sister. The same sister she had loved, and who loved her back equally, as they were growing up. She began to talk to me, her anger detectable. I knew that her pain was a direct consequence of separation. It was the pull to remain as sister-to-sister forever that was tearing them apart subconsciously.

Looking back now, it is obvious what my family and I did wrong growing up.

Following the death of my father, my oldest brother basically took on his role. He became a father to my siblings and myself. He worked very hard to support my brothers and sisters, paying their fees so they could all finish college. I was about to get into the secondary school. He took care of my mother and also made sure everybody was okay. My brother was so much like my father, both physically and mentally. He had a heart of gold. He would easily go without food or new clothes if one of us was struggling. Although he lived far way, he was always close to home in many ways. Because of his compassionate heart, God blessed him and he prospered at an early age. With everybody cared for, he decided to get married to a woman he'd met in the city he was living in. He brought his future wife to meet the family. I can still remember my mother's countenance after my brother and his fiancée had left. My mother was generally quite predictable. We could always tell when she didn't like something. Though she tried her best to accommodate the woman, we could tell that she was not a "wow" to our mother! "Mummy, you really don't like that woman, do you?" we all asked. "I don't hate her, but I just think that my son deserves better," she responded.

To us, my brother's fiancée seemed fine. We were happy for him and couldn't understand what our mother meant. "So, why do you say that, mummy?" we all enquired. She gave us so many excuses at the time. Looking back now though, I realise that she was not ready to let go of her son. She made her feelings known to my brother and he explained his future wife's attractive qualities that drew him to her. "Mummy, if you get to know her, you will like her," my brother affirmed. My mother simply nodded her head, and that was where they left it. I believe that, at the time, my mother hoped he would change his mind and choose another woman. She probably thought this because my brother was the kind of son who always listened, he was her favourite and they were very close. But to her surprise, my brother came home a month later and said, "Mummy, we have picked the date of our introduction. I need you to get the family together and come with me to ask for the hand in marriage of my future wife, in accordance with our culture." My mother was shocked and not happy at all. However, she really didn't have much choice, other than to go along with her son's wishes. We, on the other hand, were happy. We loved celebrations, especially our cultural marriage celebrations. As far as we were concerned, this was a time for feasting; where you could eat with nobody questioning you. So the wedding celebration came and went.

Commonly in our culture, your mother in-law or sibling would live with you in your matrimonial home. I was part of this back then and, not knowing any better, couldn't see past it. I couldn't see what was wrong with this set up.

My mother made sure she kept her distance, although, my brother would visit us whenever he could, and helped in every way possible. However, things were not the same following his marriage. Understandable, you would have thought. My mum blamed my brother's wife for everything he did wrong. It was always all her fault, though my mum never said as much to my brother's face, it was always said behind his back. My mum often took out her pain and suffering on us whenever she was in that moment. I knew she was displaying the characteristics of a mother's grief at letting her son go. Her emotions were pure anguish resulting from the separation a mother naturally encountered.

I had three brothers. My mother was close to two of them, and treated them similarly. My other older brother, who she'd left as a little child before she married my father, was different because she hadn't been around him much as he grew up. This suggests that bonding, and the time invested in a child, plays a key role in hindering the acceptance of a change in our children's or sibling's lives.

Jesus, despite him knowing it was time for His disciples to be separated from him, would not let go. At Gethsemane, he returned to them three times, each time playing on their emotions for his position.

This phenomenon has caused problems in families all over the world. It introduces a rift between parents and siblings, leading to a great deal of pain amongst family members. I am also a mother, raising my own children, and I cannot even contemplate parting with them, especially my sons. But I know that God is preparing me for when that time comes.

I saw my sister struggle with separation when her daughter chose to marry a man she didn't approve of. My sister was used to being in control. She'd raised her children single-handedly, and made them who they were today. Given this, she had high expectations of what her daughters should become and the kind of partners they'd have. This was the life that she wished for them. Yet, our parents never taught us how to handle the pain of separation when it surfaced. It happens to every family. Yours may be different to mine, but it does happen.

Naturally, we assume that, when we turn twenty-one, we leave home and everybody will be happy that we've grown up. Despite this though, the bond and the position within the family still remains strong. Therefore, unless you know how to adapt to the reality, that your sister, brother or daughter has moved on in life, you will end up in the pool of pain. The knowledge you possess is all you have to work with. The issue arises from the fact that we have always believed that family members will always be a part of our life, and us a part of theirs. Just as our parents hadn't been taught, we weren't taught. This is likely to continue until we turn to God and ask Him to teach us. Only then can we start to teach our children, for them to pass on to their own children and so on. This will help break the cycle of pain caused by separation.

Often reality, or the truth, is not always founded on assumptions or beliefs based on the obvious. Despite a physical separation happening, the psychological bonding between siblings remains. When that breaks, it may appear to be joyful externally, but it can attract everlasting enmity. Excited by the prospect of a child's wedding, parents often invite the whole world to their son or daughter's wedding. They are overjoyed that their son is going to start his own family, and their daughter will be with her husband and start a family of her own. That sounds like something to celebrate, doesn't it? The pain of separation, however, is deeply rooted and not physically manifested. But it is there. This is what we were never told.

God told Adam and Eve that, "If you eat from that tree you will die" (Gen.2:16). However, they did not understand what death meant. When Eve shared God's words with Satan, he told Eve, "That's not correct, you will not die". Yet, God did not inform them that if they ate from the tree, they would become mature and independent, ultimately separating them from Him. The pain of that separation would be similar to the pain of death. Adam and Eve died spiritually because they were completely separated from God.

That is what we are facing today. Growing up, we were told that getting married will make our parents happy. That is fundamentally true, but the pain of separation eventually gets in the way of their happiness. It rears itself when our parents try to go back to the life they've inevitably been separated from. That is when the pain subtly creeps in. Consequently, a lot of homes have been broken. Divorces, resulting from the fact that the mother struggles to let her son go, and the father struggles similarly with his daughters, despite being in agreement to the marriages, are quite common. They are understandably reluctant to give up their former lives, which is no longer theirs. This is where the pain of separation stems from, and we are left to deal with the agony of that pain.

Jesus's mother and brothers once came to the place where he was teaching the multitude of the word of God, hoping to speak with him (Matt.12:47-

49). His response was not what you and I would call honouring your mother. I want to talk a little bit about this story. It was written in the bible for a reason. From our perspective, it does not demonstrate the good side of Jesus ... it is not a good reflection on man. As a mother, I put myself in Mary's position, although her story is a little bit different from mine, because I didn't become pregnant by the Holy Spirit. Mary went through, what we call, shame in her time. She was chosen by God to carry the saviour of the world in her womb, her life was put on hold for nine months. The bible led us to believe that, at some point, Joseph, her fiancée, secretly planned to abandon her when he found out Mary was pregnant. He struggled to believe her story when she told him, and because he loved her and didn't want to disgrace her publicly, he decided to leave her secretly, as what Mary had done was an abomination in their culture. God intervened and spoke to Joseph, you know the story. Mary went through morning sickness, unable to do the things she loved to do. She carried Jesus in her womb for nine months, went through the pain of labour, and delivered baby Jesus. From that day, she nurtured him, fed him, clothed him, sat by his bed when he was teething and in pain, cried when he cried, and laughed when he did. In the public eye, Jesus was now the celebrity of their time. The son every man wanted, miracle working Jesus, multitude followed when he moved from one city to the other. Jesus had it all going for him.

So on this occasion, when his mother and brothers came to see him, possibly after not having seen him for days, as he was always travelling from town to town, preaching the gospel, and hadn't been home. It's possible that his mother heard that he was teaching somewhere near home and decided to pay him a visit, probably because she was missing him. We don't know what the situation was. We were just told that Mary and her sons went to see Jesus.

"Your mother and your brothers are here to see you," said someone.

"Who is my mother?"

"What did you just say, Jesus? Who is your mother? Are you losing your mind? Are you insane? Did you even hear what you just said? What has gotten into you? Have I become that kind of a mother to you? Is it because you are now a celebrity that I now become nobody to you. I told myself that if any of my children treated me like that … I brought them into the world … I will take them down. You can judge me if you want, but that's me. Are you kidding me? The child I raised will not acknowledge me because he has now become somebody. Nah! You ain't gonna treat me like that."

This would probably have been the reaction of a normal parent, but we weren't told that Jesus's mother reacted like that. You may think that she wouldn't react like that because she already knew that Jesus was going to deliver mankind from their sins; she knew he would have to do God's work. It's alright to say all that. Yes, she had an idea of what Jesus would go through, but she was not taught how to prepare for that subtle separation when it came. Mothers find it very challenging to hand over their children to someone else.

The question we don't always ask when we find ourselves in similar situations to that of Jesus and his mother, is, "What could have made my son or my daughter behave in that manner?" We don't ask such questions because we believe that we have complete authority over our children, and it's not out of place to believe so. I don't think Jesus spoke to his mother in that manner in order to disrespect her, or drag her across the floor in the presence of the multitude. I believe Jesus was hoping to teach us to realise that there will come a certain time when our children are no longer children, but adults. I believe he was helping us be more aware of life's constantly changing phases. Each phase, has a different task. What might have worked as a child, wouldn't necessarily work as a teenager; likewise, what worked as a teenager wouldn't necessarily work in adulthood. We need to be more aware of this and prepare for these moments. If we don't, things will become messy and painful because we have no control over phases, only God has that control. As we don't possess this control, it's best to learn how to handle that separation when it comes. This story is also an example of us once being in sin, but saved by blood. Sinning is a phase, being saved from it is another phase. The general expectation is that one does not repeat their sin, refraining from doing the things that were done during the sinning phase.

They wanted him to still be the little boy Jesus, the teenage boy Jesus, who ran around for them, and the Jesus who went to bed when told to. This was the Jesus whose mother carried him in her womb for nine months, fed and then cared for until he became a man. They still wanted Jesus to be the "with us" Jesus, even though Jesus had already moved on to being the Jesus "with them". That was why Jesus expressed it in a very fundamental, simple way. He was probably saying, "This is a different phase, the phase of growing up has passed. The phase I'm in now is the phase for these people. A phase where mother and brothers do not connect biologically any more. It has now transitioned to being functional and focussed on destiny".

It is important for us to teach our children that it's okay to love one another; it's okay to care for each other without crossing a line, trying to fit into a space that is no longer yours. The longer we allow separation to be a matter of assumption, fewer people will be aware that the psychological bond that has kept siblings together, eventually draws them into filling a space that no longer exists. People need to be aware that, one day, they will be separated, despite being of the same parents, growing up together, living and dining together, and even sleeping in the same bed.

This is the root cause of many family crises that we see today.

Expectations are the breeding grounds for offence. Offensiveness produces rifts, rifts create tear downs, tear downs often lead to bleeding, which results in pain. If you can change your expectations, you can stop the bleeding. If you can stop the bleeding, you can stop the pain of separation. The current rift between yourself and your brother, sister, father or mother is not a consequence of their current actions, it stems from your expectations. If you had gone a little beyond the assumption that you and your siblings would naturally part, your expectations would be different and therefore, managed differently.

I had a friend, back in the days, who came from a very well-to-do family.

Nikky and her brothers were very close when we were in school. Every time I went to their house, I always admired their closeness. They looked out for each other. The boys would beat anyone who messed around with my friend, Nikky. They went to parties together, and even attended sports games together. Their bond was very strong, it was almost unreal. After we finished high school, Nikky went abroad.

Two years later, she sent for her brothers to join her in Germany. Their parents weren't worried about them as they knew the siblings would stand together and take care of each other, which was exactly what happened. Another two years later, Nikky met a guy and got married. The brothers were still single and lived apart. When I spoke with Nikki and asked how her brothers, Lamar and Josiah, were doing, I could not believe the response I got from her: "I don't speak to my brothers anymore." I was shocked. I asked what had happened and she told me that her brothers wanted to continue controlling her; how they told other people that, since her marriage, she wanted nothing to do with them and that her husband forced her to turn her back on them. They had become so jealous of each other; they were like strangers. When the brothers got married, they didn't invite her to their wedding. They didn't even introduce their wives to her. So I asked, "What does your mum and dad say about this?" Her response was: "Oh! My mother fully backs my brothers, it's only my dad who supports me. My mother didn't try to fix this, she tried to manage us. Whenever my parents needed our help, they'd call us individually. Of course, I stood alone with my husband. I still can't figure out what went wrong." As she told me this, she was crying, and though I was miles away, I could feel her pain. She was the only girl in the family. Nikky continued, "It was so bad that, once when my brother saw my husband on the high street, he crossed over to my husband and started shouting and cursing at him, making fun of the way he looked, blaming him for what had happened between us. When my husband ignored him and tried to walk away, my brother pulled him back and started hitting him, which then led to a street fight. Oh! My word! Did that really, or can that really happen? Mope, I don't even want to hear their names being mentioned. I don't want to have anything to do with them; I don't want to see them. As a matter of fact, I don't care if they live or die." When she said that, I went silent for a very long time. "Are you still there, Mope?" she asked the silent line. I said, "Yes, I'm still here, I just can't believe what I'm hearing." So I decided to see if I could help resolve the issue. I spoke to each of the brothers individually, firstly to hear their own side of the story, and secondly, to determine how I could help rebuild the bridge that had been broken between these siblings. I tell you, the hatred they felt towards each other just didn't make sense to me. The brothers' hatred was not only towards Nikky, there was hatred between the brothers too. I saw envy, I saw jealousy, I saw pride, I saw conflict of power, and I saw competition. Everybody seemed to feel superior to the other. It was so bad that their own children, natural cousins, didn't even know each other. Oh my goodness! I had to be careful about mentioning Josiah when I was with Lamar, and vice versa; I also had to watch what I said about Lamar and Josiah when I was with Nikky.

When I went home on vacation, I went to see their parents. To my surprise, Nikky's mother was rather supportive of the battles between her children. She'd never accepted the man Nikky had married, she believed her daughter had brought someone inferior, someone who did not meet their so-called family standards, into the family. Due to this, the brothers believed that Nikky should be cast from the family, simply because she married the man she loved. The father was also in trouble with his wife because he did not support her views about the man Nikky had married, so the house was on fire. The family has been divided because they weren't aware of the pain of separation, a phenomenon they weren't prepared for. I came to the conclusion that the trouble started when they went their separate ways, each forming their own new life. The fact that they didn't see each other as often as they used to, and no longer knew what was happening in each other's life but wanted to know, all exacerbated the situation. They'd all been hanging onto this unnatural ownership of themselves. Their parents claimed ownership of the sons and daughter, the siblings claimed seniority, "Because I'm older than you, you must do as I say, or follow my instructions," forgetting that they were no longer children, and may have formed other relationships that the family may not necessarily approve off. They were not prepared for this form of separation. The belief that they would always be together brought about the kind of pain that none of them had bargained for. If they had been taught by their parents that someday, at some point in their life, they would all have to part and lead different lives, I bet they wouldn't be in the dilemma they were in now. My friend, you cannot assume that we will not feel the pain of separation. Separation is like a cut. The time you invest towards understanding and dealing with it will ultimately determine the outcome.

Previously, I mentioned Adam and Eve not knowing what it meant to die. When the time came for them to separate, they didn't know that that was what God meant when He told them that they would die if they ate the fruit from the tree of life. They didn't know that it wasn't a physical death, but the pain of separation. They were independent of God, but dependent on themselves. Carrying the consciousness of His absence would be their pain, a pain that was just as bad as death. This is what they were unaware of.

This is exactly what Jesus did for us. He brought us back the conscious knowledge that he would be with us, but also created the space for God to fit into that eternal space that separation had created. Adam and Eve did not physically die from eating the fruit. No, they were separated. A separation that brought them sorrow. This is the psychological power that families, parents and siblings, are exposed to. This, in turn, brings them to become enemies for life. Why? Because they lack the truth behind "the changing times and changing spaces". There are two things you need to do. The first is to recognise when it's time to free yourself from the guilt of "I was not there for my brother or my sister", simply because you believed that they were your responsibility for life. That is not the way God intended it. Secondly, you need to know that there are some people who will forever want to hold onto that space, and not allow others in, others who could add more value to your life, because you both came into the world through the same channel. Your brother will not always be there for you, but that's not a crime. You just need to realise that that phase has changed, and that simply means that it's time for you to let go. He's got a wife and children, colleagues, and friends. He has a responsibility towards these people. You must allow for healing in your separation, whatever the scar is. It isn't your fault that you weren't aware. If you had known, you wouldn't have allowed so much bleeding. So, now that you know, it is important that you don't feel guilty for the rest of your life. Look at Jesus, he did not hold back when he told his mother and brother that this was not a relational thing, that there was a functional purpose and that it was destined. It didn't change the fact that they were his biological family, it just meant that their assignment was over. Don't get me wrong, your love for your son and a daughter will always remain, but the best way to maintain that love is to not allow the bleeding from separation become psychological. Don't try to re-establish the bond as it will only increase the pain. As this is a natural occurrence, the time you had to bond as children is no longer available. You can't fill that space anymore.

The most powerful separation experienced by most people is that amongst families: sibling separation and parental separation, not induced by divorce or any other external factor, but purely through natural progression in time. Again, we weren't prepared to understand the impact of this or its effect on our future. As we move into new phases of life, someone will still want to come along. In some cases, you start to neglect important people in your life, such as your husband, wife or children, because your parents won't let you go. You've got to shake off the guilt, and free yourself from this form of manipulation. It's difficult for you to function in that space. Please note that it is important that you continue to love and care for them, but you cannot continue with the guilt; don't let them take you back to the place you've moved on from.

Chapter Two
The Journey of Destiny

Let me talk to you about destiny. Destiny is the journey that you make in life. It's your own journey, and your destination will ultimately bring you fulfilment. The steps in the journey will always have people who will come along and people who will drop away.

The element of confusion arises from the belief that people will, or should, always journey with you, all the way to the end of your destiny. Unfortunately, it doesn't work this way.

The ultimate destiny is yours, and yours only. People will not necessarily remain with you throughout the journey. They serve the purpose of being contributors. And guess what? Their departure could easily trigger a distraction. There is a pre-determined length of time for them to remain with you in your journey. When this time is up, when they have finished their purpose in your journey, they will depart. You can't change this, you can't stop it and you can't influence when they depart either. It doesn't matter who they are: be it your father, your mother, siblings or friends, even colleagues at work, neighbours or church friends. Either because of life, circumstances, persecutions, tribulations or death, people will drop off.

I was born into a polygamous family, whereby my father had two other wives before he married my mother. He never told my mother that he'd been married before. It was only after my mother had married my father that she discovered that he'd been married to a woman, then divorced her because my stepmother's parents had never accepted my father's upbringing in a village and his poor family background. Subsequently, his mother brought another woman to him from the village, someone who was not his ideal choice. But, he was obliged to obey his mother. So when he finally met my mother, who was beautiful inside and out, and well educated, the woman of his dreams, he didn't have the courage to tell her that he had baggage. My mother, for all she knew, had married the man of her dreams too. My mother, who already had a child before meeting my father, didn't want to end the relationship. Besides, she was madly in love with my father. He was, after all, a handsome man of great height. Who wouldn't want to hold onto a man like him? From what I was told, the love between them was very strong.

My mother went on to have two boys and three girls with my father. I was the youngest, and the last one to be born. According to my mother, I was not planned. She was done having children, but God was not. So here I was, turning up in my family. Six months after I was born, my mother met some doctrinal Christians, who led her to Christ. Instantly, her life changed. She was wrongly advised. She was told that she was in the wrong relationship, that she was an adulterous woman and marriage to my father was a sin. Therefore, if she really wanted to hang on to Jesus, she must leave everything. If you are a born again Christian, and are reading this book, you will have an idea of what I'm talking about. In Jesus, my mother had found her new lover. There was no way that Jesus could enter your heart without you feeling his love; a love that brought peace within yourself, one that is difficult to explain. She was told to leave her husband and children and stand alone. She was not only brainwashed into leaving her family, but they also persuaded her to throw away all her gold jewellery, including her wedding ring, because they were mere possessions, and she could not serve God with mammon. My innocent mother listened to them and walked away from us, leaving me, at the tender age of six months, in the hands of a house maid. She left a note to my father saying that she'd found Jesus and was not ready to trade him for her husband and children, something she later regretted.

My father was devastated. She was his world and they'd had a great relationship. He believed they'd be together until death separated them. He didn't know how to do anything; my mother ran the household. She did everything from cleaning to cooking, cooking to ironing, ironing to taking care and running the family, and she also planned his day for him. My mother was in charge from the time my father got out of bed in the morning to when he went to bed at night. She covered everything; she was a super woman according to my father. They always had breakfast together before he left for work. My father didn't know how to operate a kettle, let alone make a cup of tea. My mother was everything to him.

So, here's a man who can hardly take care of himself, who's now faced with the challenge of taking care of his children. Though my older siblings were able to take care of themselves, none of them knew how to meet the needs of a baby. There was no manual to follow. When I cried, my father cried. He simply didn't know what to do, plus he was facing the agony of losing his soul mate to some man called Jesus. That was something he just couldn't handle. I mean, if Jesus was a physical man, my father would have known how to handle the situation. The mere fact that it was Jesus, added to his pain. He grew up knowing God and was never told that Jesus took people's wives, and never returned them.

So I grew up with my father in this environment. My father was the best man who ever lived as far as I was concerned. He was the only one I ever knew. He was both my father and mother. As a road engineer, he travelled a lot. Wherever he went, I went with him. When my father retired, I was almost eight years old. That was when my half-sister came to live with us, and we both became his carer. We were the last two at home, the rest were away at college in another city, far from home. I was a daughter and, simultaneously, a mother to both him and my baby sister. He was my world. He was my hero. My father could never do anything wrong in my opinion. He was flawless. Likewise, we could do no wrong in his eyes. We were the best children in the whole world to him. He had the spirit of a dove. I never saw my father arguing with anyone, never saw him angry. We saw nothing but the goodness of his heart for people. He was also a comedian by nature, always cracking jokes.

Despite my young age, I went to the market to buy food for us to cook and eat. I learnt to cook because of my father. There were two things my father always said: he told me how much I resembled my mother, and how great her cooking was. He also told me that he'd never eaten outside when my mother was around. So I made up my mind, I would dress like my mother so my father could heal from the pain. I also taught myself how to cook, until I was as good as my mother. One of my thoughts from those days was: "What can a seven-year-old cook that anyone would want to eat?" But that was not my father. He gladly ate my food, however it was cooked, never complaining and always praising me. If we had visitors, he told them that I was a good cook. Can you imagine that? My passion for hospitality was nurtured through the process of taking care of my father.

Life was good, everything was alright. I felt safe wherever my father was. He was the perfect dad, one that would do anything for his children, he loved us to bits. We never felt the absence of a mother. Two months before my thirteenth birthday, my father got a call from his cousin, who had a project that he wanted my father to help him manage for a few months. At first my father turned down the offer as it meant he would have to leave the city where we lived; he didn't want to leave us. With persuasion, and because we needed the money, he took the job. He left my baby sister and I with my big brother, who had just finished college. The arrangement was that he would come home every weekend, which was fine. Things worked out, money came in, my father came home every weekend, things were going great, we were very comfortable, and I mean very comfortable.

It's Friday today, and daddy is coming home. We waited all night, but my father didn't come home. Saturday, we were all outside expecting daddy to show up at any moment. I mean, this was very strange. He'd never let us down before. My father was very good about keeping the promises he made to his children. You could set your watch by him. Back in those days, we had no telephone, and no means of contacting him to find out what was wrong. A million thoughts crossed our minds as children. We thought he may have had an accident, or maybe his car had broken down and we couldn't get anyone out to help him. Or had it been stolen? We waited all of Saturday, but there was no sign of my father. On Sunday morning, my uncle, the one my father was working with, sent a man to our house. He told my baby sister and I to go to our room as he wanted to talk to my brother alone, which we did. I will never forget that day. My brother screamed so loud our neighbours came running over, wanting to know if all was well because we were a quiet family. They'd never heard noises coming from our house before. It was something I was not prepared for, had never thought of. Something that had never crossed our minds during all the guess work around why our father wasn't home yet. My father had died in the early hours on the Friday he was meant to come home. He'd had a cardiac arrest in his sleep. Unfortunately for him, and for us, he died alone in the apartment he was staying in. Somebody saw his car on Saturday morning and wondered why he was still there as he'd never spent the weekend away from his children. The man then banged on the door and received no reply. So he went around the house to see if he could see anything through the window. That's when he saw my father on the floor in his bedroom. He then broke the door open and found that my father had been dead for almost two days.

Oh my God! Did my whole world crumble? Yes, it did. My whole world had turned upside down. I passed out. When I regained consciousness, reality materialised: the journey of my life had come to an end. I would never see my father again. The world became a place of pain. The father I thought would always be there, was now gone. The father that was supposed to see me through to the end of my destiny was gone. Not because of a choice he had made, it was just his destiny. I couldn't understand why. It didn't make sense to me. How could such a great man leave his children without even saying goodbye. I was hurt. I was angry. I was mad. I was wounded. I blamed my uncle for the death of my father. If he hadn't asked my father to help him, perhaps my father would still be alive, and I wouldn't have had to go through the pain of losing him. I didn't stop there. I turned on my mother for walking away from him. If she had stayed, he would have still been alive. I never forgave my mother. God was not off my "to-blame" list either. I not only blamed God, I cursed Him, if that was possible. I even hated the word "God" for a very long time.

Now, I ended up with my mother. The woman who had abandoned me when I was a baby. The woman I never knew. I knew she was my mother, but it was difficult for me to accept her as my mother. My resentment towards her was at its peak, but I had no other choice. The man I loved was gone, and I had to accept my fate.

I was in so much pain, I couldn't eat for days, when normally I ate about six times a day. I loved food; food was my soul. But now, food felt like poison to me. I refused to eat because I thought I could starve myself to death, and death would take me to my father. I couldn't sleep either. I would sit by the window, watching the stars at night, expecting my father to just drop down from heaven and come home. In the event I slept, I'd wake up and run straight to my father's room, expecting him to be on his bed, but that was an illusion that never formed itself. I can still remember the times when I stood outside our house, or walked down the street, every man I saw looked like my dad. There was one time when I came out of our house and saw the back of a man walking past. I ran across the road because he looked so much like my dad from behind. I almost got hit by a car, but when I approached the man, I realised it was not my father. You can only imagine what that day and week was like for me. Then, I thought I heard a woman ask my mother whether my father had ever come to her in her dreams. It was the best thing I'd heard since my father had departed from this world. I mean, wasn't it wonderful to know that the dead actually came to you in your dreams. So I was happy, felt comforted with the belief that when I slept that night, my father would come, or at least, could come. So, I went to bed early that day, hoping to meet my father. It didn't happen. I looked forward to sleeping every night, only to see him. I had so much that I wanted to share with him. I wanted to tell him to come home, tell him how life had become so unbearable without him, how much we missed him, and that if he wasn't able to come back, could he take me with him? But guess what? I never saw my father in my dreams. That depressed me even more. My father was supposed to be with me through every step of the journey to my destiny. It was hard to let him go. It was too much to give away. In all of this though, looking back, one thing that made God real to me was that, through the pain in my darkest hour, God accompanied me in my journey. He did not, not even once, let thoughts of committing suicide, in the hopes of seeing and living with my father, enter my mind.

I believe God took me through this journey so I would be able to help you, if you are going through the pain of separation, or others who have gone through, or are going through certain phases in life. Like those who have lost their loved ones, those whose parents weren't there when they were growing up, or those whose parents have abandoned them, or just don't care or don't want to know. Or someone whose husband walked out of their marriage for another woman. Or your wife left you for your best friend. Or you're pregnant and your boyfriend, who loved you, left because you were pregnant and you feel like life is not worth living.

Maybe your own situation is different to my own. Perhaps your mother didn't abandon you, but your father did. Yes, death did not take your father, but the prison did. Or perhaps prison didn't take your father. Instead it was an illness or drugs. Whatever your situation, people dropped out of your life at a time you least expected them to. You couldn't understand why, you couldn't comprehend it, but they left you with a pain that you've been carrying for a while, and no one understands, or feels, that pain the way you do. You need to know that … it's your journey, it's your pain, and it's your destiny … no one else's.

When people depart, your journey doesn't end. I will say that again. When people depart, your journey doesn't end. People's departure will not stop your journey. I never thought I would live a day without my father. It's now been thirty-six years since my father died, and I'm still alive. Remember that time you were in primary school, and you were about to go to the secondary school of your choice?

You probably wanted your closest friend to go to the same school, but they weren't accepted. Perhaps their grades weren't good enough or perhaps the school was full. That would have saddened you because your best buddies wouldn't be joining you in your next phase of education. Did that stop you from going further academically? Perhaps you know of someone who did stop because of this, but I've never met anyone affected to that extent. The truth of the matter is, the time you spent together in primary school was only supposed to be for that period of time, and that phase in life. At the end of that period, you were meant to part with them. You were meant to let them go, regardless of whether that was your choice. It wouldn't matter who, or what, they were.

This is where the pain begins, that point when you fail to realise that people will never understand, or feel, your pain. The pain worsens when your expectations are for people to understand or feel your pain. What happens next is that you find yourself wanting to hold on, and you start pushing for them to understand your pain, hoping things change and they return to you. Oh! How I wish I knew this in my early years. The abuse I suffered at the hands of men wouldn't have happened. My inability to let go of my father resulted in so much pain. I can't even begin to explain how much. I was completely messed up. My head was messed up. My mind was messed up. For a very long time, I sought the love of many, and in the process, they abused me. I was desperately looking for someone like my father, to fill the void within me. I searched for someone to understand my pain, but no one did, not even my mother could feel my pain. You know what, because I held on to a father who was gone, I couldn't move on with my life. There was a time when I ran away from my mother for days. I travelled thousands of miles to stay with my brother in the city because I didn't want to be with my mum. I refused to continue with my destiny and had wasted so much of my life because of my inability to move past my pain.

Maybe that's you. You've got to trust God and move on. It's important to let go of those who have departed. If you don't, it means you're stuck where you are in life, and you will stagnate. It's also important to realise that there are some who are not meant to travel with you. There is a chance they could hinder you if you forced them to journey with you.

"Moreover whom He predestined, these He also called; whom He called, these He also justified; and whom He justified, these He also glorified." Romans 8:30

This basically means that the foundations of the world are pre-set. They cannot be changed by anyone. So hanging onto things that God has already set in motion is like running on treadmill without a destination.

"They went out from us, but they were not of us; for if they had been of us, they would have continued with us; but they went out that they might be made manifest, that none of them were of us." 1 John 2:19

For every stage of the journey, there are various people who play specific roles. My friend, unless there is a void to fill, the right person cannot fill it. More importantly, there are phases during the journey that you can use to re-group and re-gain your strength. The friend, the partner, the father, the husband, the boyfriend, whoever has left you, was not given the power to voyage with you in your journey of life. If they were meant to do so, they wouldn't have left.

When God was ready to take me through my second phase, He took my father away and brought my mother back, though I hated it. Oh My God! I don't even know this woman well and you're going to leave me with her? I didn't want to be with her, didn't feel safe around her, never trusted her, even though she could be trusted. I rebelled against her, hated her, just name it, I had it in for my mother. But I was in another phase, one God had predestined, and she was positioned to walk with me to my next phase. She forcefully taught me the way of the Lord. She taught me morals, taught me how to pray, taught me how to trust God, the God I didn't want to hear about, the One that took my father away. My mother planted seeds that would bring forth its fruit in season, "the word of God" in me. Oh! How I hated it, hated going to her church. It was a nightmare from my perspective, but it was planting time for my mother. She never stopped shoving Jesus down my throat, whether I liked it or not. But today, I thank God that she didn't give up, that she didn't join my pity party, but focused on the assignment that God had given her: to make me aware that there was a God who could take away pain, heal the broken hearted and set you free. The kind of God that would never forsake you when others did. Though it was tough, through my mother's prayers, He saw me through my hard times, held my hands, became the light in my darkest moments, wiped away all my tears, and filled me with His joy.

Joseph's journey to his destiny is another example (Genesis 37:12-36,39-46). He was taken away from a father who'd loved and cared for him. His brother stripped him off the home he had always known. He was sold to a foreigner and taken to a completely new environment. A place where he knew no one. He'd never left home before, but now he found himself amongst strangers from a different culture. Oh! It must have been really tough for him. He thought his journey to his destiny would include his father, but it became a nightmare. He didn't know what the future held. A boy who'd been born with a silver spoon in his mouth, became a slave over night.

What a wicked world we live in. The truth is, the journey of life is hidden from you. You can't know it, can't see it, can't feel it, but you have to walk it alone. Euuuhh! Lord have mercy. The thing is, both Joseph and his jealous brothers had no idea what God's plan was. None of us do.

"For I know the thoughts that I think toward you! Says the LORD, thoughts of peace and not of evil, to give you a future and a hope." Jeremiah 29:11

That is why, when Joseph's pressing time was over, he was able to tell his brothers, "What you meant for evil, the Lord has turned it to good." He said, "Though you thought it was over for me, my God says it isn't. The Lord actually sent me ahead of you to preserve your life." This is why you have to put an end to your pity party ... nobody else is going to feel your pain.

And then they joined him at a place called **Gethsemane, according to the bible** — which translates to Oil Press — (Matthew 26:36). Jesus had taken them to the place of press ... it is true that they came with him, but they could not stay with him ... **many people can come with you, but not many people can stay with you** ... but if God comes with you, He will stay with you ... oh yes, if God comes with you, he will stay with you.

That is why he said, "I will never leave you nor forsake you ..."

That was why He said, "If you are in the fire, I will be there with you." Many can come with you, but not many can stay with you.

I admit, there are phases of your journey to your destiny where friends, no matter what their level of friendship, cannot come with you ... it does not matter whether they are comrades, constituents or confidants, according to Bishop T. D. Jakes — there is a point in your journey where only God can feel your pain ... Not your mother, your father, not even your wife or your husband — when your pain is beyond human capacity — only God can feel your pain.

Jesus brought his disciples to the place of Press and separated them by level.

He told them to "sit here while I go to pray" ...

Jesus was on his way to pray. Of the eleven, he asked eight to sit and three to join him ... as they moved further away from the eight, it is obvious how quickly he split out the confidants (those who are there for you) from the comrades (those who are there because you are there).

This is what you and I always fail to do ... when you are unable to separate your confidants from your comrades, you want everybody to feel your emotions the way you do, often getting upset at those who are unable to do so. No, they were good for the communion table at the penthouse, but they were not capable in the confidence of the place of prayer …

As Jesus moved to the next level, he was pressed with emotions, fear and agony. He was dealing with a serious inner pain and had no choice but to share it with his three confidants — Jesus took them further and said — ***"My soul is exceedingly sorrowful, even unto death: stay here, and watch with me"***.

The Creator stripped himself naked in the presence of the Created. This was Jesus, the son of God, the eternal rock of ages, the king of the storm … now telling his confidants that, "My soul is sorrowful even unto death …" Not sorrowful because of the cross, the cross he knew of before he came, but rather his sorrow came from the pain of separation. He did not want to be separated from the people he had built and moulded; he didn't want to be separated from the people he loved so much. But if he didn't leave them behind, he would have terminated the journey to his destiny.

You would have thought that Jesus would have the ability to deal with his own problems, without having to pour his sorrowful heart out to the three — but that was his confrontation … *Unless you can confront your weaknesses, you will not command your strength.*

A lot of us bottle up our problems until we become emotionally derailed. We pretend and cover up our weaknesses and fears until we lose our strength ... but Jesus opened up to his confidants.

The question I asked myself when I read this emotional statement from Jesus to the disciples is, why would the leader speak out with such emotion, one that could be painful to those who loved him so much?

I quickly realised that they saw him in his glory, they saw his healing power, and they saw him in his anointing. But he wanted them to see him in fear ... and that was what got me. They were sensitive to his glory — to the extent where Peter said, "Let's stay here forever." They were sensitive to his anointing, but **do you know why they couldn't feel his pain?**

No one can feel your pain if they're not accompanying you to where God takes you next ... they lack the capacity to fill the space. So, Jesus realised they couldn't feel his pain and told them, "Stay hereafter, watch with me," and went along, dropped to his knees and prayed ...

You see, you must learn to move past those who don't feel your pain, to the place of conformity, where it is just yourself and God ... you cannot hold onto those who are unable to help you at this stage — you need to be in that place of intimacy, where it is just you and God.

Commonly, we have the tendency to hold on to our confidants, even when they cannot come with us to the next level. This is simply the nature of the highest level of human relationships. That was why Jesus demonstrated human nature in this drama — the natural tendency to disregard something that pulls us up, reverting to that which pulls us down.

I asked myself, why in the world did Jesus have to keep returning to these disciples? Three times he left the place of prayers, only to return to his confidants, leaving the super confidant — God — to return to human confidants — men.

Each time he returned, he realised they couldn't feel his pain. If they felt his pain, they'd be watching; if they felt his pain, they'd be praying; if they felt his pain, they'd be awake. But each time he returned, they were all asleep.

They came with him but didn't stay with him … many people can promise to come with you, but not many can stay with you …

What! Could you not watch with me for an hour? I don't think Jesus was surprised at finding them asleep — Jesus knew what was coming in the days, months and years to come; he knew what would befall them because he knew what the guilt was going to do to them. In this sense, I think Jesus was asking them a hypothetical question — **Do you know why, you can't feel my pain?**

They can't feel your pain because they can't go where you're going.

They can't feel your pain because they don't necessarily have the tenacity to stay with you.

They can't feel your pain because you are moving to your next assignment level ... whenever you move to the next level of your destiny, you cannot hold onto the previous level.

Don't get angry or upset with people when they can't feel your pain. If they have what it takes to feel your pain, your pain will be their pain. They can't give you what they don't have. They can't come with you to your next assignment level if they don't have the capacity to take the pain. Don't get distressed by this, or get worried over them. It is important to understand that if you can stay in your place of conformity, you will soon have your confirmation.

"Then an angel appeared to Him from heaven, strengthening Him." Luke 22:43

Think about it. Do you think that, if Jesus had had the companion of men, the ministering Angels would have ministered to him? I don't think so. The reason for this is that God wants to be in control of your life. As long as you keep holding onto people, closing the space to Him, He won't be able to help you. He cannot be replaced by anyone; no one can take His place. He has full custody over your life.

Every time the wrong people are permitted to sit in that space in your life, you will never have the right people filling it. And the longer these people spend in that space, the less value they will add to your life. You trying to force them to stay will make no sense, and will actually cause more upset than you expect. You must understand that people will never understand your pain when the journey to your destiny is so pressing. This is because they have never been where you've been, never walked your path, and they are certainly not going where you are going, so stop letting this get to you. All things are working together for your benefit.

When Jesus disconnected himself, he literarily put the disciples in a permanent state of sleep so he could free himself. He wasn't going to return to them as he'd already told them they could sleep. He brought a closure to this part of his life, creating the space for angels to minister to him (Luke 22:43). One of the things about God is that He has a way when all help fails. He does this when people think you have been displaced, or when you yourself think that you have shifted from the place of your dreams. In reality, you have not reached there; you are just in-between.

"Finally, there is laid up for me the crown of righteousness, which the Lord, the righteous Judge will give to me on that Day, and not to me only but also to all who have loved His appearing..." 2 Timothy 4:8

When the bible refers to a crown being laid, what is the bible telling us?

Jesus was enjoying the freedom of clicking his fingers and getting what he wanted without much resistance. For instance, Jesus had the pleasure of calling upon Peter to set up a place for them to eat supper. Another instance is when he told Peter, James and John to loosen the colt and bring it to him. When Jesus moves, the multitude follows. He has the power to heal, the power to raise the dead, and the power to deliver people from the oppression of the devil. People worshipped him, bowed down to him, and even the sea obeyed him. Walking as a man in his human form, the ease of things made him seem like he had forgotten why he was chosen to walk this journey alone. One of the things you must not do is confuse the beauty of the journey with the end of the destiny.

Chapter Three

Under the Shadow of Separation

Yea, though I walk through the valley of the shadow of death, I will fear no evil; For You are with me; Your rod and Your staff, they comfort me ... Psalm 23:4

The fear of losing what you have can seem as painful as experiencing loss itself when we don't trust God with where we are in life. Sometimes, we become so over protective of our current state, we tend to be blinded to the beauty of greater things ahead. Trusting in your comfort zone is one thing, but trusting in the place of the unfamiliar can be challenging. The thought of the loss of separation can cast a heavy shadow of pain on us. The future then seems really bleak and gloomy, but God has a way of shedding a light to aid us as we break through our fear of separation, lifting us from our lows to reach our highs.

My story may seem strange when you get to know it, but unless you share my experiences, you will never know my pain … life can be tough, but God is always good.

My husband and I, with three of our children, lived in South Yorkshire, in the north of England. It had been a year and half since my husband left the United States (US) to join me in the United Kingdom (UK) — what a love! That year and a half had been very difficult for my husband, who finds the UK challenging to reside in. He was used to his big house and fuller life in the US. The house we bought in the UK seemed like a mansion to me, being an English girl, but resembled a box to my husband, who complained day in, day out. However, he would not trade his family being together for anything. We'd been apart for a long time, and that was something we never wished or prayed for again.

Though my husband didn't like the UK, we had managed to settle, and the family was solidly grounded and bound together in our cosy beautiful home.

It was in the heart of winter, in 2008, when my husband received a phone call from a recruiter. A phone call that changed our lives forever. As soon as he ended the call, my husband's eyes lit up, and his demeanour lifted. I was very curious about the call and the effect it had had on my husband. My husband doesn't get excited easily. He is not the kind of man who expresses his positive emotions freely. Even in the moment of the most fascinating story, he will tell it as though it was nothing exciting. But this time was very different. He was clearly filled with such happiness. I asked him what this was all about — my husband won't tell you the full story from the start when it comes to something like this, he never gets straight to the point, keeping you in suspense when you're desperate to know. I think that is the Preacher in him! His answer made me curious … he said, "I think I've got a job coming." Then I said, "OK!" I thought he was referring to a job in the UK. So I asked him, "Since when have you been looking for jobs. I thought you liked your current job?" That's when he gave me the little piece of information that made me curious — "I wasn't looking for a job," he said, "but I think this one is going to be a great job." That didn't tell me much … "I really would like to know what kind of job in the United Kingdom would get you so excited. So excited that you have this joy all over you — can you share?" I said. You know how some people can get you worked up and keep you guessing, well I really don't like that. At this point, since my husband wasn't very forth coming, I started to suspect that he might be thinking of leaving us and going back to the States. So I pressed further until he said … "It is a job in Dubai." I sighed with relief. That really sounded good to me. I'd never been to Dubai before, but I'd heard a lot of good things about it. I asked if we'd all move to Dubai and he said, "Of course!" Well, the unfortunate truth of the story was that the job wasn't actually in "Dubai".

It was only when the company flew him out to Bahrain for an interview that it was revealed that the job was actually based in Saudi Arabia. He told me on his return from the interview. That made me seriously depressed because, surely, my husband had placed the financial gain, his career progression and senior position over the considerations of our family's Christian beliefs, and our allegiance to Christ. We were both church lovers. My husband is a Pastor, one who has Pastor churches for many years, even when working full time as a Food Science professional. We had just initiated a little gathering in our home, with the intention of starting a church. Our Sunday service at home was already something our children looked forward to. And now, we were to go to Saudi Arabia? That did not sound like God to me, plus I wasn't going to give up my freedom to live in the dark age. I wouldn't be able to practice my faith as a Christian; my children would not be able to go church, let alone grow up in church like their parents did. I just couldn't understand why my husband could not see what I was seeing. And I didn't know how to tell him what I was feeling without sounding like a selfish woman, one who didn't care about her husband's success. My husband was not thinking about the freedom I'd lose though. Based on what I'd read on the internet, women weren't allowed to drive. I was used to driving myself to wherever I wanted. Furthermore, women weren't permitted to dress the way they wanted.

You had to wear the long black thing over whatever you were wearing. Also, there were no public buses, so women were completely restricted. I wondered how on earth I could live in such a country! While I was battling with the potential loss of freedom and separation from my place of comfort, he was glowing with the joy of a new beginning. He was ready to go to Saudi Arabia, but I wasn't ready to leave my place of freedom. So I started praying. I prayed for God to not open this door, and prevent my husband from getting this job. This was not God's will, I said. Well, the more I prayed, the better the offer he got. There was no way he was going to walk away from this great tax free offer. There was only one other person who could help me talk to him, and convince him that what he was planning to do was not right. That person was our Pastor and he was also my husband's spiritual father. So I picked up the phone and called him. I told him what my husband was considering, how he was going to sacrifice Jesus for money; I went on lamenting. The man of God listened until I'd finished. He then asked if I was done. I said yes. When he next spoke to me, I was shocked. He addressed me as "my anointed daughter" and went on to tell me how God had told him that God was sending us to Saudi Arabia as secret agents. "You've got to be kidding me, right?" was my response. He said, "No, I'm not kidding you. That's what God told me." Although, as he'd not been given a specific timing, he wasn't certain whether this was the time referred to by God. I must have asked the man of God more than three times whether God had really spoken to him; in the end I put the phone down. I had no idea what God's plans were, but from that point onwards, I started to say, "Lord, if this is You, I will go wherever You want me to go."

God will separate you into a vacuum. If He closes one door, He will open a better door ...

"For my thoughts are not your thoughts, neither are your ways my ways, saith the LORD."
Isaiah 55:8

When God wants to detach you in order to help you rise, you will never see the full plan. The more I researched about Saudi Arabia, the more I asked God, "Are you sure you want us in this place?"

This memorable phone call later created a landmark in the life of my husband and I. My husband was given the job with an offer that, in all his years in the food industry, he'd never experienced. Our family were going to be comfortable, our children would go to one of the best International schools in Riyadh, it sounded very good. He jumped on the offer and signed all the paper work. His start date was sent to him and he couldn't wait to leave. Of course, just like most employers, a passed medical was required, not just for the company, but as a pre-requisite for a residents visa in Saudi Arabia. So we drove four hours to London so my husband could have the medical done. I guess it wasn't just me who didn't want us to go to Saudi Arabia, the devil wanted to prevent this too.

I remember arriving in London at about nine in the morning. About four o'clock in the afternoon, my husband returned to the car, where I'd been waiting for seven hours. His demeanour had changed. He looked exhausted. "Are you okay?" I asked him. He then handed me the paper he held in his hand and told me to read it. I began to read what was written and read something about carcinoma. I had no idea what that meant, so I asked him what it was. And with this sorrowful heart, and a shaky voice, he said, "It means that I've been diagnosed with cancer in my lungs." So, let me put this into perspective for you … you came to obtain a visa for what you considered the best thing that had ever happened since cheesecake. But now, instead of a visa you're served with venom. Hard to believe and difficult to conceive. How can you have lung cancer if you've never smoked in your entire life? Something is wrong somewhere. The report must be wrong. I knew right then that the enemy had crept in. Surely the devil was already in place to stop us, and God already had his verdict of victory written all over the journey.

My world crumbled. Have you ever been in a situation where the unexpected happens? Though you hear it from people, you never thought it would ever happen to someone close to you, especially not your husband. Have you ever been at the peak of your life, when everything you'd worked hard for, prayed for, and put all your effort into ... meant life was going so smoothly that you enjoyed waking up every morning, and because you were so happy, you'd thank God every day. Then all of a sudden, all of that was going to be taken away from you.

Thousands of things went through my mind. How was I going to raise my children without their father? Would I have to be at other men's mercy to survive? Throughout my journey, this was the only man who'd treated me with respect, believed in me, trusted me, loved me, a man who would do anything for me. Where would I go from here? What would I do? How would I survive without him? How would the children handle this? God, this could not be happening. I mean, the devil put all sorts in my head that day. It was like a death sentence had been declared on my husband. Suddenly, I heard a voice from within me say, "Declare it upon him, 'you will not die but live.'" So, from deep within, I started declaring the words of God on him as I drove us back home. During the four-hour journey home, my husband only spoke once, and that was only in response to my question, "Baby, why are you not talking to me?" He said, "I will be talking to you alright. I will have to show you where everything is, the insurance and all the rest of it." He then went silent. I knew immediately that the news had hit him hard because my husband was someone who could and would talk non-stop. He was trustworthy, and never repeated a word. You could count on him anytime you wanted to off-load whatever was on your chest. He was a talker and a listener.

That night at home was like hell on earth. He couldn't sleep; I couldn't sleep. He was on the internet all night, reading more about the diagnosis, whether it was curable, and how many had died of it. He looked at how long people survived after their diagnosis and what the symptoms were. He read all sort of things. While he was on the computer downstairs, I was upstairs in our bedroom, crying out to God. Throughout my entire life, the longest I'd ever been able to pray for was an hour. On this night, I was on my knees for seven hours and didn't even realise I'd been praying that long. You can just imagine the pain I was going through. My first marriage had been when I was in my mid-twenty's, a marriage that I referred to as one you "don't wish on your enemy". It was a marriage that was violent from start to finish. I knew that marriage was wrong for me from the beginning, but I refused to admit that and kept on believing it would get better. I thought I'd make it better, but that never happened! I used to cry in bed every night, asking God for a way out of that marriage. Eight years later, God finally gave me the courage to walk out of that marriage. The way things had been going, I knew that man would kill me. And now God had given me the right man and cancer would take him away from me? God forbid. That was something I just could not accept

The diagnosis was one thing, my husband's job offer was another. We had to let the company know what his diagnosis was. If you had any medical issues, the Saudi Arabian embassy would not issue a visa for entry into their country. This added to my husband's pain. However, something was weird about my husband's thinking process during this time. He would not quit talking about the job. He lamented about the job he was losing, and I lamented his life that I'd lose. At one point, I told him, "Fight for your life and let this job alone." His world was shattered. He'd lost his appetite for everything.

However, the Saudi Arabian company was very supportive. They were willing to hold the position open for him until he'd completed his treatment, which was a relief for him and also for the family. This meant he could focus on getting all the treatment he needed, and still be able to take up his new job.

The medical journey began, one of unending tests and surgeries. Finally, they came up with a chemotherapy treatment plan, following which my husband said to me, "Honey, I am not going to do no chemo. I'm going to trust God to heal me." I'd read online about how chemo made people feel sick. "I'm not going to take chemo. We are just going to believe in God for a miracle," he told me. I was glad that he'd said that. I had waited for him to join me in prayer to stop this evil. One morning, while he was recovering from his biopsy surgery, he was lying in bed and I was in the kitchen downstairs. He called my cell phone because he was in pain. Shouting my name from upstairs would have worsened it. I quickly ran upstairs to help him. To my surprise, he was watching *700 club*, and Pat Robinson's son was giving a prophetic word. He said, "There is a man watching on television. You have just had an operation because you have been diagnosed with lung cancer. But the Lord said, 'He is healing you right now, go back to your doctor and have it checked.'" I jumped up and ran around the house like a crazy woman. I had received the prophecy. I believed the word of the Lord and I held on to it. To my husband, it was too good to be true, so he asked for another X-ray to be done. However, it came back with the same diagnosis. But I believed the report of the Lord and began to encourage my husband to be strong and stand on God's report. If you are reading this book and you have been diagnosed with any kind of disease or have been given a set time to live, I want you know that there is power in the blood of Jesus. Don't focus on what the report says, listen to the words God is saying. Declare it, confess it, pronounce it, keep saying it until it becomes the breath that you take. Trust in the power of His name. Believe His report. I know that the facts say, "You have this or you have that." Yes, the facts are there, but the facts do not necessarily determine the final outcome. And if God says you are healed, you are healed ... *"But He was wounded for our transgressions, He was bruised for our iniquities; The chastisement for our peace was upon Him, and by His stripes we are healed."* Isaiah 53:5 NKJV.

So accept your healing in Jesus's name.

It had been six months into this painful journey when, suddenly, my husband received a call from his hiring manager. He was told that the CEO of the company was putting pressure on him to hire someone else for the position as they weren't sure whether my husband could make it to Saudi Arabia and they couldn't hold the position open any longer. They were going to start interviewing other candidates for the job. My husband of course was upset at the news, but there was nothing he could do about it. And you know what? He never gave up on that job to my surprise, and truthfully, to my annoyance.

It was about a few weeks later when I got a phone call from my husband while I was at work. He said, "I've got my visa!" "What visa?" I asked. "The Saudi visa, of course." "At least it's good for you to lift up your spirit. So that sounds like a good joke and as they say 'claim it' in church stuff — right?" I commented before continuing, "It is time for you to give up on this job in Saudi Arabia and start thinking

DO YOU KNOW WHY YOU CAN'T FEEL MY PAIN?

of something else. God will do it in His own time, if it is His will." That's when he said, "That's what I'm trying to tell you. He has done it. I have a Saudi visa on my passport as I'm speaking to you. Miracle!" So right after I'd left for work that morning, my husband had jumped in the car and headed off to the visa office. He had not driven since his last surgery, so I never expected him to take the risk of driving four hours with cuts in his lungs. I just could not imagine it. I asked him how he'd managed this. He said the Lord had prompted him to go and talk to the visa doctor. All he asked the doctor was why they were delaying his visa. He'd had the surgery done, so he requested his visa. The doctor couldn't believe what she was hearing and not wasting a second, she ordered my husband's visa to be issued immediately.

This is the God I'm talking about. The God who does the impossible, the God who doesn't need human approval to do what He wants, the God who is not a respecter of persons, the God who promotes, and no one has the power to demote. When He chooses to bless, no one can curse. When He opens a door, no man has the power or ability to shut it. I have never seen this kind of God before. Have you?

Well, it was one thing to have the visa. It was another thing for the company to have an open vacancy for him. Therefore, my husband had to call the company and inform them that he'd been issued his work visa to Saudi Arabia.

Now, what God did, truly blew my mind for the first time in this whole journey. The very same day that my husband's visa had been issued, was the same day the company had planned to send an offer letter to the new person they'd considered for the position my husband had been delayed for. His phone call couldn't have been made at a better time. His future boss was happy, as he'd come to like my husband and was hoping he'd recovered enough to join them. The other guy never received his offer letter and the rest is the story of us in Saudi Arabia. We knew it had been the devil that had tried to prevent us from going to our place of purpose. God had turned our mourning into song. Whatever your situation is, heed His words: ***"Then you will call upon Me and go and pray to Me, and I will listen to you."*** Jeremiah 29:12 NKJV.

If you continue to trust God, He will turn your pain to joy. He will make your heart rejoice again. Though sorrow may last for a night, joy will come in the morning. Your problem is not too big for Him to solve. His hand is not too short to lift you up from the pit of trouble, depression, suffering, or whatever is affecting you. He is a loving and caring Father, He hates to see His children suffer and is waiting for your call. Go ahead, call on Him.

Chapter Four

Building the Memories
that Build the Pain

*"I will go before you and level the exalted places;
I will break in pieces the doors of bronze and cut
through the bars of iron"* ... Isaiah 45:2

When you consider Sarah, who gave birth to Isaac under a memorable, record breaking scenario, defying medical science, it's best not to offer Isaac as a sacrifice ...

It is what you have achieved, the success you have acquired and the fruits you have produced in a place or in a person, that forms the memories that will result in the deepest of pain when you become separated from that place or person. This is often the reason why people are reluctant to become attached ... because they don't know how to say goodbye. Good memories are the outcome of a good investment.

What God did with us in Saudi Arabia may one day become a documentary, one the whole world will marvel at when they read or watch. My husband is shying away from telling the story, but my life history in the realms of the joys and the sorrows has no better place to express itself than here. I have built memories that will surely overwhelm me with grief when the time of separation arrives.

Three months after my husband had left to Saudi Arabia, I arrived there with my children. I'd had these months to settle my mind and open it up to adapting and enjoying whatever God had planned for us in Riyadh. As soon as we'd settled down, I started to ask God, so what's next Lord? We are here because You want us to be here, so, what's up, God? We started worshiping at the British Embassy, as it was the only place to worship without being harassed by the religious police. The worship at the embassy was a gentle, catholic/orthodox kind of worship. We ourselves were Pentecostal, "happy clappy", lively church goers. My children and I did not get much fulfilment from the service, but it was somewhere we could meet people from various aspects of life, so we continued attending for social purposes. The British Embassy became the place that prepared us for what God intended to do with us in this country. It got to a point where socialising was not a priority; I wanted more than just meeting the same people every week. We eventually found an underground church, a community of Filipinos. It didn't matter who they were and where they came from, all we knew was that they were born again Christians. Their worshiping was in alignment with what we believed a worship should be. So we started to worship with them. Our souls were being fed and we became a family, though most of the time they spoke their language. But that was okay, our spirits were connected. The Holy Spirit has a way of interpreting, and most times somebody would interpret for us.

In Saudi Arabia, most western expatriates live in compounds surrounded by walls, with a high level of security. Likewise, we also lived in one of these compounds. I reached out to all Christians in our compound and we started having bible studies. My husband is a great teacher of the word, so he led the bible studies. More people started to join us, and before we knew it, the numbers had increased and everyone had fun in the presence of God. One day, at the end of one our bible studies, as our Filipino church Pastor and his wife were leaving, and as we passed the recreation hall in our compound, he said, "You know that, one day, God is going to start something from this recreation. I don't know what God wants to do, but He surely has his eyes on this place." That was it for me. I'm the sort of person who looks for God's voice everywhere and I disliked missing any such moment. In the time we'd lived in Saudi Arabia, I'd asked God about this scenario several times. So when this Pastor made the statement, my spiritual eyes opened up to things we were doing and those that never crossed our minds. Later, I said to my husband, "Did you get anything out of what the man said?" He looked at me and said, "Honey, I know that your desire is to bring people together and start a church. I am not here to start a church. It will be impossible and difficult. I'm not saying God cannot do anything, but the law of the land does not permit a church. I am not going to join them in forming an underground church. I want to be able to go to church openly. I don't want you to get your hopes up too much because it's a battle that we cannot win." So I left it alone.

The passion of starting a church in an unlikely place such as Riyadh was like fire in my bones. When we were worshiping at the British Embassy, we met some Nigerians. As some of these Nigerians didn't have family in Riyadh, I asked my husband if we could invite them to our home and cook for them, and then hold a fellowship together. He agreed and one day, while we were all sat down, the Lord spoke to my heart. So I asked the Nigerians if they'd like to meet regularly, even if it was once a month, to pray together. To my surprise, they all said yes. My husband then went to speak to the manager in charge of the recreation hall. The recreation manager mentioned us to his manager and said it was fine for us to hold it once a month. And so we started having a fellowship in the hall on a monthly basis. I would wake up very early in the morning and cook hot food. I kept the food warm in the oven so we could sit around the tables and eat after the fellowship. Oh! By the way, did I mention that I was also four months pregnant? Yes, I was. People started joining us from the British Embassy to worship with us. What was supposed to be a small Nigerian fellowship, soon became an all nations fellowship. During one of our monthly fellowships, a man came and gave us a message from God, "God said, I want this fellowship to be held every Friday. I no longer want you to do it every month. I don't just want a fellowship, I want a church." OK! My husband and I both looked at each other. We had the same question, "How?" Nevertheless, we stepped out with faith and went to a shop where we spent all our money on the materials we needed for a church. We must have spent about six to eight thousand dollars on a church we had no idea how to create. We spoke to the people God had commanded us to hold church with every week, and they jumped on it. During the week, God spoke to my husband regarding the name of the church and he decided to call it Grace Outreach Church, in honour of his spiritual father. He spoke to the man of God about it, who gave his blessing. We then went ahead and did as God commanded. And what happened next? Ninety-five per cent of our Nigerians brothers and sisters left as soon as we give the church a name. They wanted it to be called the "Nigerian's fellowship". That wasn't really possible. We had followers from more than ten nations. We needed to accommodate everybody. I was upset, but my husband wasn't. He'd seen this happen before. "You cannot depend, or rely, on people when God is calling you into something big, especially Nigerians. Honey, I want you to know we are on our own from this point," he said. The more our own people turned against us, the more God sent other people to support us. News of our church spread across the city and God took over from there. We went from ten people to one hundred within three months.

The rapid growth of the church was so drastic the compound security didn't know how to handle the crowd. They started to get concerned about the Saudi's finding out that there was a church in our compound. There was a chance the compound would be attacked by anti-Christian's, potentially making the compound risky and dangerous for other residents.

I will never forget the day my husband called me, crying. I was on vacation in Tulsa, Oklahoma in the US, and about seven months pregnant. Oh my God! What had happened? In all the years I'd been married to him, I'd only heard him cry once, so I knew this was something serious. Before he could say anything more, I told him to hold on and went straight to the toilet. I started throwing up and became short of breath. I panicked then as I'd forgotten that I was seven months pregnant, and that I shouldn't haven't put myself in that state. But

I couldn't help it. I had left my children with my husband. With him crying, of course it was natural to panic. After a few minutes, I pulled myself together, picked up the phone and asked, "So which one of them is it?" "Which of them is what?" He asked. "I know of nothing that will make you cry if it's not your children. So I'm asking, which one of them, and please don't lie to me. Whatever it is, I can take it." "Honey, nothing has happened to our children," he affirmed. I sighed with relief. Oh God, thank you. "So why are you crying?" "We have been stopped from holding church in the compound, and I don't know what to do. Honey, this is why I didn't want to form a church, because the country itself is a big barrier." "It's alright," I said. If God called on us to do this, He has a better plan. It's very important to remember, firstly, who is in control and who has given you the task. Secondly, when one door closes on you, it is important to remember that God has bigger plans. It doesn't matter how hopeless it seems, always believe that He wouldn't call on you to do something, then take His hands off. God does not operate that way. *"He who has started a good thing shall complete it until the day of our Lord Jesus Christ"*.

We stepped out in faith again and rented a tent close to our compound. It was situated on a street in an open place. Christians in Riyadh gathered to worship in fear, because of their own experiences and what they'd seen the religious police do to their fellow Christians. Now God was asking us to gather out on the streets? It sounded like an impossible mission. My husband and I walked by faith and not by sight. God gave us the courage to walk this way on a daily basis. The people's courage grew daily and their fear slowly started to diminish. It was difficult, but we were strengthened by the power of the Holy Spirit.

We also decided to start a choir. My husband was the Pastor, the drummer, the pianist, and the choirmaster. On Friday's, he would take the instruments from home to our place of worship. I was the cook and cleaner. Our twelve-year-old and I, along with another mum and her daughter, were the singers. It was so funny. You might be wondering why we held our service on Fridays. That was simply because Thursday and Friday was the weekend in Saudi Arabia at the time. During every service, my husband would be on the keyboard to start us on the right note, then he'd run over to the drums and play them until we moved on to another song. It was tough on him.

Our American brothers and sisters started offering their villas for the Friday worship as the rented tent began to get too small for us. We ended up moving from villa to villa. We became a "moving tabernacle". Around this time, the father of one of our brothers was due to arrive in Riyadh to visit his son.

As he was a Reverend, we thought he would be able to help encourage and strengthen people's faith, simply by having someone from another country, especially America, preach to them. So we started to make plans. The villas didn't have the look of a sanctuary, but the tent did. We decided to rent the same tent we'd had before. Everything was set, people were expectant, we were excited and looking forward to this new move of God amongst His people. Three days before the Reverend was due to arrive, my husband's heart yearned to go back to the tent, just to make sure that all was well. My husband called the man, Pastor Dominic, who'd passed on God's message about starting a church. He'd been with us since the day God had passed on that message, and had been my husband's right hand man all along. They both went to the tent, together with another guy Pastor Dominic had brought along with him when he'd joined our church. When they got to the tent, they couldn't believe their eyes. Cows were in position to be slaughtered, the tent was decorated, clearly in preparation for a big party. What on earth was going on? We didn't do any of this or request it. Finding the man in charge, they asked what was going on, informing him that we were scheduled to have a gathering this coming Friday and had just come to check all was OK. The manager just looked at them and double checked that it was the coming Friday they needed the tent. My husband and his companions confirmed this but the manager informed them that that would not be possible as the tents owner was having a big party there on Friday, hence all the decorations and the camel. In Saudi Arabia, if you weren't an indigène, you had no rights. There was nothing my husband or his companions could say or do that would change things, so they walked away, with no refund. The money was not our biggest concern, it was the venue itself. We really needed a venue for Friday. We were expecting a lot of people to arrive to meet and be blessed by the Reverend from the States. What were we going to do? We would rise above this. Were we going to trust God as we'd always done? Yes, we would. One of God's attributes is His ability to raise people whenever He chooses to. Sometimes, this would be done so subtly, if you didn't trust and have faith in Him, you would easily miss this happening. He makes things seem hopeless. Every door that He had previously opened would become difficult to open, or not open at all. God has a way of completely taking your hands off His glory sometimes. When all your efforts are exhausted, He steps in.

My husband and his companions then drove around the city for hours, looking for an alternative venue, with no luck. They decided to go back home and work on a plan B. On their way home, they passed a building, a beautiful building. It was a building the Arabs frequently used for special occasions, like weddings. My husband suggested they enquire about availability there, saying, "you never know." Pastor Dominic hesitated slightly. Even if this place was available, it would be too expensive. My husband, however, was the sort of person who "sees the importance of money, but puts God first". "Let's see what it is first, then we'll decide on what to do," he said. As my husband couldn't speak Arabic, he let Pastor Dominic do the talking. "We want to know if this place is available this Friday?" Pastor Dominic asked. "Yes, it is," the man replied, "what is it for?" "We want to do Salah." Salah, is prayer in Arabic. "Ok, no problem." "How much is it?" Pastor Dominic asked. "Five thousand riyals." Or one thousand five hundred dollars. As soon as the cost was mentioned, Pastor Dominic said, "My Pastor, the place is available, but the money he is asking for is too much." "How much is it?" my husband asked. "Five thousand riyals." A while ago, I'd given my husband five thousand riyals to buy something, he still had the money in his wallet. As this was the amount being requested, he looked in his wallet and found the exact amount in his wallet. "We will take it and we will pay for it right now," he said. With our venue secure, God was glorified. We hosted our guest and the church was packed with people being blessed. Subsequently, we started to use this venue for monthly services. Every offering we collected went towards renting the place. The church grew in number. People started contributing towards supporting the vision God had given my husband. Before we knew it, the building became God's tabernacle and we started using it every Friday. We held our first year anniversary thanksgiving at this venue, it was an awesome occasion.

The caretaker was a Muslim, a hard-core Muslim. One day, he told us that he wanted to take two thousand off the five thousand in light of the fact that we were only praying . If we'd rented the venue for a party, it would have cost no less than seventeen thousand riyals, yet we only got it for three thousand. Do you still doubt this great God? You'd better not. He is the only God who does the impossible. Just try Him; He will blow your mind.

It was in the morning of the March 15th, 2010, when something strange happened. It set up the course of our church for good in Saudi Arabia. It was an amazing story, one you will find hard to believe.

"Good morning, Pastor Victor," a colleague greeted one morning. "Good morning. How are you today?" "I'm fine, sir." A few hours later, there was a knock at my husband's door. "Can I come in?" "Sure." It was one of his colleagues, an American who'd lived in Saudi Arabia for a long time, also a converted Muslim. As he shut the door behind him, my husband offered him a seat. He sat down and began to speak to my husband, "I heard that guy call you Pastor Victor this morning. Are you a Pastor?" "Yeah, that's why he addressed me as one. So, is something the matter?" The man replied, "No, no, no. It's just that some government officials are looking for someone who would stand for Christians in this country. The officials have spoken to many Christians, but no one is interested in doing it. They all believe it's a trap. Seriously!" My husband was naturally unafraid of challenges, "I will give it a shot," he stated. "OK, I'll talk to the officials and arrange a meeting with them." And that was how God opened up a new chapter in our journey.

The date was set for my husband to meet these important people. They consisted of Islamic scholars, the head of religious police, and the chief Imam of Islamic affairs. This is how the story went …

LOOKING AT THE OVERVIEW OF THE MONUMENT …

In 2011, the Lord opened a big door of favours to us so we could have, what I called, "A one of a kind Holy Ghost revival". It was the first revival the country had ever witnessed. That sounded amazing! Right? It surely was a wow! But a wow that came with big challenges. My husband had spoken to the government about Christians gathering together, and it had been approved. They told us to apply for the permit that allowed both men and women to congregate together. Saudi Arabia is a country where men and a women are segregated. It was against their religion. A woman could not be in the presence of a man who was not her husband or her brother, on her own. Even in restaurants or food courts, segregation applied and there were women and family sections. Anyway, we went ahead and applied for the permit. It was granted. We had requested we use their football stadium due to its immense space and its location in the centre of the city, making it easy enough for people to get to. When we went to view the stadium, the manager told us we had the capacity for twenty-five thousand people and, for acoustic purposes, we'd be better off aiming for that number, otherwise the sound would just feedback. There was no way we'd reach that many people, so we gave it up. My husband then requested the Riyadh Sports Centre, which could accommodate ten to fifteen thousand people. This request was granted. We then invited Christians from all around. Churches from across the country all came together. We printed out badges with people's name on them and the logistics were all in place. It was strictly a Christian event, Muslims were not allowed in. We made sure we'd covered all the necessary things and ensured no Muslims were allowed in. Those were the orders given by the government and we had to ensure we followed the rules, or they'd stop the event. I'd never seen so many Christians together under one umbrella, all eager to reinforce Jesus in Saudi Arabia. To many, it was an impossible venture. To some, it was an answered prayer. To others, it was a "we will believe it when we see it" scenario. But that had nothing to do with the issue we encountered.

Just two weeks before the event, there was a riot that broke out in the region. The country was in serious chaos. News of the revival had spread rapidly; it was known in everybody's home. The Saudi's had also heard about it. There were more people against it, with only a few who weren't bothered. Given the situation, the government re-evaluated their decision and the risks outweighed the benefits, so they considered either stopping us altogether or postponing the event until the riot had died down. Use of the Sports Centre was terminated. We ended up, figuratively speaking, jamming the phone lines. We needed to find a venue that could accommodate five thousand people at least. If we found one, we decided we could do two or three services. I was lucky if I got to see my husband before nine p.m. each day. He usually left home at six in the morning. He was a miracle and worked tirelessly. Despite a lot being at stake, it was more important for him to be able to offer this to Christians in the country, Christians who'd just started to overcome their fears, Christians who'd been praying thirty years for a revival to take place in Saudi Arabia. We contacted just about every venue and eventually found one: The Four Seasons Hotel. It had all we needed, the location was good, so we went to negotiate. We eventually agreed on two hundred and fifty thousand riyals, the equivalent of sixty-six thousand dollars, for one day. That sounds extremely expensive, doesn't it? Yes, it was quite a lot of money for a venue, but the church of God had grown to the point where it could afford to pay this sum. We informed people that the venue had changed. Two days before the event, we received a phone call from The Four Season Hotel. They said they'd been informed that the event was a Christian one, so therefore, due to security concerns, they couldn't let us use the hotel. So we requested a refund, which they refused. Why did they refuse? "Because your permit didn't say this would be a Christian event." They said this was an Islamic State, one where there was no regulation that allowed Christians to do such things. How were we to get a permit that specifically stated that? Even if we could, it was Wednesday afternoon when we'd received the call from the hotel. The weekend was Thursday and Friday. The government offices would be closed. Oh! I'd never seen my husband so drained. "Two days to the revival." What were we to do? People had started arriving, from the US, Europe, Syria, Jordan, Dammam, Jeddah, and even Egypt. As leader and organiser, what would you do in a situation like this? All we could do was go back to the One who'd sent us. When I heard the news, I said to my husband, "God is behind this. He is talking to us and we are not listening to him. If we're not listening to Him, we can't hear." My sister, who'd come from Maryland in the US for the revival, and I went into a room and started praying, asking God to lead us to where He wanted us to have His revival. For a moment we got carried away with our excitement and claimed the revival as our own, rather than His, and He called that out to us. It was like we heard God say, "By the way, guys, this is my revival, and you are all acting like you are making it happen. I call the shots, not you." We acknowledged our error and He said, "I will direct you to the place where I want my name to be lifted high and glorified." He then led us to the building where we had our first year anniversary. We had our first two day celebration in this building, and had the thanksgiving in the temple, our regular place of worship. "God, you do have a great of sense of humour," I said to myself. How would this place hold eight to nine thousand people? The whole story was like the story of Jesus's birth. He didn't get the inn, nor the palace, he got the barn. "Not our will, Lord, but your will." None of us were comfortable with the place. The planning committee were still trying to find venues, but none were to be found. God's choice in venue was the only place available in the whole city, and believe me, there were hundreds of them. All hands were on deck. People came together to clean the place and transport chairs from every corner of the city. A lot of people did not get much sleep, they worked all night to get the place ready for the revival the next day.

The 2011 revival was finally here. The worship came from the throne of God. Having all churches come together under one accord to lift the name of our Lord Jesus high brought about the glory of God. His presence was so heavy, you could feel it. It was a beautiful revival. God showed himself off. We had two services, with each service serving four thousand people. I never got to attend the Azuza revival in California, but based on what I'd read, I can tell you that the 2011 Riyadh revival was a mini version of Azuza. Healing was the meal of the day and hundreds of people gave their lives to Jesus. If you have ever driven past a football stadium at the end of a match, you would have an idea of the kind of traffic we had to deal with going home. I'd never seen anything like it.

Chapter Five

The Vision that Attracted the Attack

Jesus answered and said unto them, "Destroy this temple, and in three days I will raise it up." ... John 2:19

Those who carry the sword, which can separate you from your purpose, can see the future better than you can. The level of threat you pose will determine the intensity of the attack you get. The magnitude of your vision will always be the only thing that attracts detractors to your journey.

My pain came from being separated from something that will forever be called a "barrier breaking" and "line crossing" venture ... the building of the largest **"over the ground church"** in Riyadh, the capital of Saudi Arabia. "A church in Saudi Arabia?" Yes! **A life changing, breath-giving and people-making church** in the heart of an Islamic nation! But the attack came from the vision of wanting to do far more than renting a place to create a church, it was to do with persuading Saudi Arabia to allow a centre that could be called the Centre for Christianity and Culture.

The more God opened up doors for my husband in the government, helping him form better relations, the more his appetite to take the church to higher grounds grew.

It was not that different from the statement Jesus made to the Pharisees — informing them that he could do the unusual. The more Jesus talked about the opportunities, the more enemies he attracted. My husband was almost like that. He was on fire and just wanted to see God move, but the bigger is vision became, the more intensive the attack became.

The church grew from two hundred members to six hundred. People were flooding in from different nations. We now had twenty-nine nations worshipping under one name and one umbrella ... Jesus. God started bringing in people who were experienced and gifted in running a church. A structure was put in place. Now we had both the business and the church side set up. It was starting to feel like a church that the world would actually call a church. We had ordained six Pastors to lead different ministries in the church. We went ahead and rented a property for sixty-six thousand dollars a year to hold our weekly activities, as our place of worship did not have a building large enough to accommodate our weekly programs. People were willing to cover their area of expertise, so we all put our hands together and the Church of God blossomed.

Through the grace of God, my husband formed a good relationship with the government, which put us in a position to obtain visas for the men of God, from all over the world, to come and minister to people in Saudi Arabia. Within a year, we were bringing a minimum of four ministers of God to Riyadh for our annual church anniversary. There was one year where we had about six bishops from the US and UK come to Riyadh. All travel expenses, hotels and honorarium when they left was paid for by the church. It's obvious how God had boosted His church and how it was now flourishing.

We then started to stream our service live. This was supported by a company in the United States that we'd used to train our media team on how to use the software we'd purchased from them. The software enabled people to watch the service online, which was an upgrade and forward move for the church. Six of our Pastors were sponsored by the church to attend the Bishop TD Jakes Pastors and Leadership conference to increase exposure, and be better informed through the enormous Church Management and leadership talk that Bishop Jakes gave at this great conference.

One day we went to see one of our American members in hospital, who'd just had a baby. We started talking to her husband, who was a lawyer for a law firm in Riyadh. He said, "Do you know that you can approach the government for land to build a sanctuary?" My husband's face lit up. "Really?" was his response. "Actually, I can help you write the letter when you are ready." That was it, my husband took him up on the offer. He spoke about this to the leaders in the church. I'm sure that when he was speaking to the leaders, they were probably thinking, "Is this man out of his mind? I think he is over ambitious. It is a mission that is impossible." Some were supportive, while others had reservations. One of the things I like about my husband is his ability to ignore negative comments. He couldn't stand being around people who were comfortable in their own little kingdoms, especially when he was receiving clear instructions from God. So they wrote the letter and sent it to the Mayor of Riyadh, who then transferred our request to the governor. My husband was then invited to meet the governor of Riyadh, who then promised to pass the letter to the late king, King Abdullah. Meeting upon meeting commenced. While all of this was unfolding, we created a fundraising account and called it the "Hope For Riyadh". Luckily for us, the wife of the lawyer, who'd suggested we request land to build a church, was an architect. She created all the architectural plans based on my husband's vision of what the future church would look like. The "Hope For Riyadh" was intended for all Christians in the country. It was not for Grace

Outreach Church members alone, it was for all nationals. The intention was to help all the other underground churches come out of their hiding places and worship freely in their various languages. The goal was to unite all Christians. My husband called a meeting with all the underground church Pastors to inform them of his plan and share his achievements with the government to date. We were going to raise the funds needed to build the facility. None of the underground churches were asked to contribute towards the building of the facility. Primarily, my husband didn't want them to think he was asking them for money to build a facility under his own name, thereby eliminating thoughts of him using these Pastors. My husband had been building and Pastoring churches for decades, so he knew the kind of thoughts that went through people's minds whenever money was involved, so he was very careful with how he handled the situation. When the meeting with the Pastors took place, their response was exactly what he'd expected. Some thought it was a great idea, others saw it as my husband trying to build his own kingdom. There were some who saw it as a ploy to scrap all underground churches so our church would be the only one recognised. Some Pastors also thought this had nothing to do with God's will, that it was just a matter of our own "ego". The Pastors' perceptions were incredible. These were the same people who never thought the 2011 revival would go ahead, but God proved them wrong. However, they'd seen enough to believe that if God was aligned, anything was possible. Faced with all these negative comments and unsupportive perspectives, my husband did not get distracted, instead he was even more driven to reach his goal. This was largely because this plan was not just for this generation, but for generations to come. Actually the more they rejected the vision, the stronger it got. Also, his vision was further motivated by the fact that a lot of people in our church had bought into the vision and were looking forward to the day when God would give them a place, some place where the world could see that the earth was the Lord's, in all its fullness. People were contributing significantly and we were all ready to see His glory come down in this "Hope For Riyadh".

After a year and half, King Abdullah finally received our request and gave the order for his own two sons and his half-brother's son to facilitate the project. He gave them instructions to provide us with some of his own land, not the government's. A fee was required to pay for registering the name and a certain amount was contributed towards the approval. The rest was secretly sorted by King Abdullah. King Abdullah had already done a lot to try and bring Christians and Muslims together for peace. He'd also started a program in Vienna, Austria, called "King Abdullah Interfaith Initiatives". My husband was invited to speak at one of the events of the King Abdullah Interfaith Dialogue, with the late Prince Sultan who was the Crown Prince, to speak on behalf of Saudi Arabia in 2011. He sat together with the Vatican representatives, and with diplomats from other countries. During this event, the late Prince Naif talked about the same desire King Abdullah had: to bring the Muslims and Christians together. I believe God was mentally preparing us to have a building for Christians in Saudi Arabia, so when we knocked, the door just flung open. King Abdullah was a man who loved peace. Arrangements were made to take my husband to view the land the King had allocated to us, but my husband had no idea what the purpose of the meeting was. On arriving there, the princes, one of whom was the Deputy Governor at the time, the other the future Minister of Interior, communicated what the King had ordered them to do and that he could see the land. But the future Minister of Interior was not pleased with the King's decision. He had no choice but to obey the King though. As my husband was leaving, he looked him in the face and said, "You've crossed the line, Victor," and walked away. My husband could tell he wasn't happy about the situation. Although, my husband couldn't understand why he was upset, he wasn't too bothered by it. It didn't matter how and what he felt, we had the land. It was too good to be true. "You have the land to build a church in Saudi Arabia?" Didn't the bible say that the heart of the king was in His hand? Only He had the power to take it where He wanted. This couldn't be. It didn't sound right. No, it didn't. Isn't that why my God is "The Almighty, the God of the universe"? When God wants to do something, no one, and I mean no one, can stop Him. He blew everybody's mind. I will never forget the screaming and shouting that erupted when my husband made the announcement to the church during one of our yearly conferences, "the gathering of the glorious". Some were rolling on the floor, some were running around the building, some cried, some danced with tears rolling down their cheeks. The praise went up and the glory of God came down.

It had been seven years since the church was formed and we'd had no harassment from the religious police. They had a tendency to go around, disrupting services, arresting people and imprisoning them. To us, God had been very good. It's not that they did not come to our services, it's just that God prevented them from embarrassing us. So many of their secret service agents had been sent to our services. They came and pretended that they were one of us, just to see if we are preaching against Islam or infusing people with hatred towards the Muslims. But each time they attended, we prayed for the King, for the land, and thanked God for giving us the opportunity to reside in this country. Additionally, my husband always preached to the church that it was important not to be part of those who criticise the religion or the people, because if God hadn't allowed that religion to exist, it wouldn't. He always made it clear that God had not sent him to preach to Muslims, but to make sure the souls of Christians in Saudi Arabia were not lost. Many Christians in Saudi Arabia couldn't find a place to nurture their soul and ultimately converted to Islam. Some literarily offered people money to convert to Islam. For those who came from poor countries, this meant having a meal in the day. They soon fell into that trap of having to trade their beliefs for money, in order to take care of their families. "These are the people I am called for," he said. Many criticised him for that, but he didn't care and carried on with the assignment God had given him. Statistics indicate that for every one hundred Christians believers who arrive in Saudi to work, twenty end up converting to Islam, and my husband was not going to stand for this

We had been unable to go on holiday together as a family for six years. My husband and I took turns to travel so the church always had one of us present. In the past, my husband and I used to spend time away from the children to have some time together, but we couldn't do that anymore because of the church. We had put so many things on hold for the church, things like spending Christmas or New Year together in another country. It wasn't a problem really. We were happy that God had chosen us to build a church for Him in an unusual place. A place where no one wanted to. A place where the name of Jesus was forbidden. A country where people were beheaded if they preached nothing but Islam. A land where Christians walked in fear. So we were grateful. The lack of holidays together didn't bother us because we knew there would come a time when we wouldn't need to worry about the church being harassed if we went away.

In August 2013, officers from the Ministry of Interior went to my husband's office and asked for him. Fortunately, he was on holiday at the time. So they spoke to his boss and told him that my husband had been converting Muslims to Christians, that he had been smuggling bibles into the country and selling them to Muslims. The officers went on to say that my husband was also renting houses to perform underground services aimed at converting Muslims. You name it, all kinds of false accusations were made against my husband. They then asked the company boss to fire my husband and deport him from Riyadh. The company boss, however, knew my husband and told the officials that someone was trying to frame Victor, that the man they were referring to was not the kind of man who'd do anything like that. The boss informed the officers that most of Victor's Muslim colleagues loved him because he never once spoke against their religion, never condemned their religion like others did, and always encouraged them to go to the mosque every

Friday. Not only did Victor encourage them to visit the mosque on Friday's, he'd follow it up at work the next day, asking if they'd gone to Jumat and whether they'd prayed for him. My husband was a well-respected and loved colleague. With this positive character profile, the officials left. My husband's boss never actually told him about the visit. He didn't want my husband to worry about this at work. The company boss also believed that one of their ex-employees, one my husband had been forced to fire due to poor performance, might have tried to set my husband up.

Six months later, my husband and I went on our first vacation together since forming the church. We went to Nigeria for two weeks. We had planned to return via London so we could attend our Bishop's 50th birthday, which we did. The occasion came and went. On our second day in London, we were driving to church when my husband's boss, also the CEO of the company, called, "Victor this is urgent, I know that you are on vacation, but I need to speak to you as soon as you're able," he said. "I'm driving to church right now, I will call you as soon as I get there," my husband responded. My husband began to wonder, what could be so urgent that his boss would need to call during his vacation? The CEO was not the kind of man who'd disturb you while you were on holiday. My husband knew this must be really important. So, on arriving at the church, he got out of the car and walked away to a quite spot where there'd be no interruptions. When I next saw my husband, he looked like there'd been a death in the family. His boss had told him that the government had made some further serious allegations against him. This time they were accusing him of selling church robes to people and shoving bibles down the throats of their people, and that he must be deported from the country. His boss had been fighting them and had attended several meetings, fighting back on behalf of my husband. This is one thing the Saudi government were particularly good at doing. If they wanted to get rid of you, they would issue the order to your employer, who was powerless to say otherwise. However, the company my husband worked for was also owned by one of the Princes of Saudi Arabia. This Prince had also tried to speak to the Minister of Interior, who'd issued the order, but the calls went unanswered.

"Boss, I am innocent," my husband assured the CEO. "I know, Victor, and that is why the Prince and I are going to try and sort this out," the CEO said with determination. "I just wanted you to know what was going on. Also, I'm not certain what they'd try to do on your return." "I really appreciate this, Boss, thank you," and that was the end of the conversation. Now, imagine this scenario: you've just heard that serious lies are being told about you, you are being framed for something you did not do, it seems like you may lose your job, and losing your job meant losing your church. No one was permitted to reside in Saudi Arabia without employment. You couldn't apply for citizenship after a certain number of years. It was a country where you couldn't get a mortgage on a house if you were a foreigner. Even worse, they were free to deport you whenever they wanted to. No notice period for any of this was required. And this was the country where we'd established a church. Having heard this bad news, if you were in my husband's shoes, would you feel like preaching to people about love? Or about any subject for that matter? My poor husband was scheduled to preach to the church at this Sunday morning's service. I was already inside with some of the Pastors who'd come to church with us. When my husband walked in, I knew something was wrong. I went up to him and asked, "What is wrong, baby?" "All is well, baby, we'll talk about it later. Right now I have to mount up the pulpit and deliver God's message to His people." That was the end of the conversation right then. He stood up and preached to the people while he suffered on the inside. No one knew of his internal turmoil. Following the service, we went out with our host and some other people from the church, and didn't get the chance to talk. My husband acted as though everything was fine, nobody sensed a thing. When the evening was over, we departed and went to our car to drive back to our hotel, which was an hour away. It was a good opportunity to talk, so I asked, "What was is it that you were going to tell me?" As soon as I'd asked the question, my husband became depressed and his voice began to shake. "The Ministry of Interior want my company to get rid of me. They have come up with different allegations against me and are pressing my company to get rid of me." "God will fight our battle," I said in response. It was much later, before we went to bed that night, when we both held hands and prayed to God, the God who had sent us and held our backs all these years. He never took His hands off us. We reminded Him of everything we had given, our time, our money, and the serious risks we had put our family through in the process of building His church. Lord, many have called us fools for risking the lives of our children for other church people, some thought we did it for the money, but we never took a penny from the church. We asked God to let the world know that He had chosen us to do this, and to not let our enemy, "the devil" rejoice over this situation. We went to bed and boarded the plane back to Riyadh the next morning. On arrival, as we went through immigration, we were stopped and taken to the immigrations office. We enquired as to why we'd been stopped. The immigrations officers started asking my husband questions, questions related to why the government may have placed restrictions on his name. Their systems didn't indicate the reason, it just said we were not allowed re-entry into Saudi

Arabia. Was this some kind of joke? "My children are in your country and you are telling me we are not allowed to re-enter?" My husband called his company and somebody from the office spoke to the immigrations officials. Whatever was said, they let us go and told us to sort this out with our employers. The world began to weigh heavily on our shoulders from this point onwards.

Back to work; business as usual. The day my husband went back to work, the CEO was away. So he carried on being as normal as he could at work. Two days later, the CEO returned to a letter from the Ministry of Interior lying on his desk. The letter stated that the Minister wanted to see the CEO, and that he was to bring Victor along to this meeting. So the CEO sent his secretary to call my husband so he could inform him that they were going to the Ministry of Interior. The last time my husband had met the Minister, he was not in power then, but he was now, and the heat was on. This is the story my husband told me: The Minister sat them down and the CEO asked the Minister why the he had been avoiding Prince Sultan's phone calls. Prince Sultan was the son of the late Prince Sultan, the late Crown Prince, who also owned my husband's company. He was older than the current minister, the Minister of Interior. So Prince Sultan had been calling the Minister of Interior (Prince Naif) to plead my husband's case and innocence, but had been avoided as he was an older uncle. Prince Sultan had no idea what had transpired between Prince Naif, King Abdullah, his sons and my husband regarding the land that was given to build the church. The Minister of Interior was not going to tell him. My husband wasn't aware of the whole issue surrounding the land either. It was only during this meeting that he began to understand Prince Naif's parting message about crossing the line. "I called you here to give you two options. Option one is to close your church and stay in Saudi Arabia. Option two is for you to leave the country with your family and your church stays," he firmly stated. My husband had a choice to make right then, and he made it. Firstly, this guy had the power to do whatever he wanted as the Minister of Interior. Most Saudi's could not be trusted when it came to Christianity issues like this. My husband didn't believe that if he chose option one, he wouldn't be thrown out of the country anyway. There was a lot to lose if he chose the church over staying in Saudi, but opted for the church. I know that God would and will fight for His church. My family and I, on the other hand, would still survive if we left Saudi Arabia. It wouldn't be the end of the world, our God had always taken care of us, and He wouldn't leave us now. Besides, this was my time to let God know how much I loved Him, and that I was willing to give Him my all. My husband chose to walk away from half a million British pounds in shares in Almarai, which was due to be cashed in eight months, along with his five hundred thousand riyals, the equivalent of one hundred and thirty thousand dollars, as a bonus for this year. He knew his family's comfort lay with the church we'd built. "I will leave with my family if you keep your promise to let the church run, so that Christians who came to your country will have a place to worship," my husband said. "It's a deal," agreed the Prince. His boss couldn't believe him. He said, "Victor, I've never seen anyone like you before. Wow! You really do love your God and Christians. I am not going to tell anyone about this." From the moment my husband made the decision to leave Saudi Arabia, the cord attached to everything we'd built was severed, and he started to bleed. But he bled alone. It would have been different if he'd bled and allowed someone to take care of his wounds, but he chose to bleed alone.

Chapter Six

Separated from the Monument You Built

Then saith he unto them, "My soul is exceeding sorrowful, even unto death." ... Matthew 26:38

What do you do when you are separated from the monument you built? What do you do when you see the marriage you worked for slip away and you see another woman enjoy the harvest of your sweat? What do you do when the woman you love is taken by another man? What do you do when the ground you are standing on, watching a great future on the horizon, suddenly caves in and buries you from your dreams? What do you do?

The grief and the sorrow that comes from the pain of being separated from the great investment you've made is always as deep as the pain of death. Unless you understand the greatness of God and His power, and unless you know who God has made you to be and His plans for your life — the separation from your greatest investment could be devastating. That is why I call it a monument. It stays in your memory, it brings back all you've invested and every element of those memories are painful.

"What God builds with you today is an introduction to what He will build with you tomorrow." I will say my greatest lesson in life comes from this knowledge.

Being forced from the monument we'd built almost sucked the life out of me, until God gave me the grace to see that He was not just a God for today, but a great God for tomorrow.

Think of how you, as a woman, gave all of you to a man, or you as a man gave all to a woman, how you put your own education on hold so he could have his, how you got the loan so he could continue learning. Then this "nobody" becomes "somebody", and just when you thought it was time for you to enjoy the fruits of your labour, the same man or woman turns around and says, "I've found somebody else". Even if this was never the case for you, you can imagine the devastation, the sense of loss and the havoc it would create. My pain didn't arise from an experience like this, but from something more monumental and historical. My pain came from something we'd built, something the world never got to hear about. Probably because we did not build for extravagance, but the story is true and real. All the wheels were now turning to get us out of Saudi Arabia. The most powerful man in Government held the sword that was demanding the head of my husband. The King, who'd cherished my husband's vision, was practically on life support, his children were being side-tracked and the end seemed near. My husband and his boss tried everything, but my husband was just exhausted. However, I kept on hoping.

One Tuesday afternoon, he came home as normal. He gave no indication that something had happened. He certainly didn't say anything but, "Honey, I don't know how long my company will be able to fight for us to stay in Saudi Arabia. Keep your prayers up, but I suggest that you start putting our things together. Let's start packing gradually and we will trust God from here." I didn't hear him tell me to start packing because I had so much faith in God. It just wasn't feasible that God would bring us this far, to a point when things were just starting to come together, then knock us down. We had the land to build the church, the world was about to hear about this great God, who had done the unbelievable and opened the door to Christians. I reassured myself that, surely, He couldn't or wouldn't do it without us. Wasn't this why He'd brought us here? Right now we were fulfilling our destiny. This was the enemy's doing, and the enemy would fall on his face when God was through with this. I was hoping, praying, and waiting to hear the outcome, not knowing that my husband had already made and closed the deal. So what was I supposed to do? What I could do was to start putting things in place. I could start allocating certain church tasks to people. What was I to say to the leaders of the church? How could I tell the church that he'd come to the decision alone?

Things started to become a reality when my husband came home two weeks later and said, "Honey, it's final." "What is final?" I asked. "It was finalised today that we will be leaving, we have been given a date to leave, and it's very close." "How close?" I asked. "In six weeks." Six weeks? What? The first thing that came to mind was the church. What were we going to do about the church? What was going to happen to it? This was the moment my own cord attachment was severed, and the bleeding began. I cried like never before. "God, I can't believe this is happening." I felt like everything we'd laboured for was about to slip away. To me, it was like a child I'd carried for nine months. After enduring the morning sickness, and all that came with pregnancy, a bad labour, being unable to have a normal delivery and having to be cut open for the baby to come out. Follow this with the pain of recovery. Then having to nurture the baby, breastfeed it, take care of it when it was ill, until the baby turned seven. Then all of a sudden, somebody tells me it's time for my baby to be given to someone else. Someone, who has never been pregnant or looked after a child. Someone who wouldn't recognise what the child's needs were when they cried. Someone who didn't know when to put the child to sleep. Who didn't know how to make the child smile. How would this child survive in the hands of a stranger? My bleeding was uncontrollable. I was bleeding so badly that no amount of bandaging could stop it. My husband had put so much into this church; we had invested a lot. It was our life. We didn't know life without it. We were attached and our members were our family. We looked forward to spending time with our volunteers every year. It was a time when my husband and I showed our appreciation for their commitment to the work of God, and for supporting our God's given vision. We enjoyed treating them as we would any prince or princess of the most highest God. We invited them to one of the finest hotels in Saudi Arabia, where a table was laid before them, where waiters waited to serve them, just as they'd served in the house of God through the year. All expenses were paid for from our resources. As the First Lady of the church, I had grown with a lot of them, especially our South African sisters and mothers, who had started the church with us. Many of them were like mothers and fathers to me. Likewise, I was a mother and sister to many others. Grace Outreach Church Riyadh was a family church. I truly had put a lot into the establishment of this church, and just when I was supposed to be enjoying the fruits of my labour, I'd been kicked out. The thought of someone else replacing me was unbearable. To me, it was absolutely unfair. How could I have worked so hard and when it was time to start harvesting, that right was taken from me. I don't know who the reader of this book is, but if you're going through something similar, or have been through this, I want you to know that I now know exactly how you are/would have felt. I really feel your pain. It's the kind of pain that no one but God could understand. If people don't understand, they can't stop your bleeding. This was what Jesus went through when he walked the journey to his destiny, the cross. He knew it was time to leave his friends of three and a half years. They had become his family to the extent that he called them his true friends. They did almost everything together. He had invested so much in them, had trained them, moulded them, but now, he had to leave them behind. He was bleeding on the inside. Though he was the Son of God, he came to us as the son of man, in the form of a human being, and felt emotions like we did. The pain of separating from his disciples was one thing the disciples weren't aware of. He knew he was destined to leave them, but they thought he would be with them forever. After all, the Torah said the Messiah would remain with them forever. They simply couldn't understand. His internal bleeding was so bad that he told his close friends, Peter, James and John, "My soul is exceedingly sorrowful and deeply distressed" But no one understood. Because they didn't understand, they couldn't feel his pain, and couldn't stop the bleeding.

Every single day of that week was like torture to my heart. Then, the spirit of condemnation sneaked in. I started blaming myself for our predicament. My husband never wanted to start a church in Saudi Arabia, but I pushed him to do it. Perhaps if I hadn't pushed him, we wouldn't have had to leave. Now he was attached to what I called an investment. The church was our investment. Anything you labour for with your time, money, and sweat, is your investment. You may be too religious to believe that, but that's OK, it's a fact. Now my husband had to walk away from the department he'd built in his company, he had to walk away from the job he loved so much, a job he gave his all to. He also had to leave the teams he'd built, both in the church and at work. His shares and the bonus he was looking forward to, something that would have secured our future, and that of our children, was something he'd had to forfeit. I felt responsible for all of this, and I became depressed. But through all my pain, I never let go of God. I needed Him to see me through, as though He was a human being, but I definitely would not talk to Him face-to-face or hold his hand. I also understood that if God was not done with us, it would have been impossible for the enemy to do what he did. Our daughter's favourite song, "God is able", gave me strength. Indeed, God is able to provide exceedingly, abundantly, and above and beyond what we ask for, imagine, or think. Don't give up on Him, it doesn't matter what you are going through, though it sounds, looks and feels like you won't make it, please don't give up on Him. He will never give up on you, because He is able.

We had made a home in Saudi Arabia. How was I going to pack everything in six weeks? We had more than just one suitcase worth of possessions. We'd acquired a lot of things over the seven years we'd lived there. How were we going to sell our cars? Our son was scheduled to sit his GCSE exams. We'd just renewed the tenancy agreement with our tenants in the UK. Where would we live in the UK? Question upon question ran through my mind. My pain intensified. I cried to God and asked him all sorts of questions imaginable. Why was He taking us through this pain?

My husband and I discussed how to manage the whole situation without creating fear in the heart of the leaders. You don't need a prophet to tell you that if they can get rid of the leader, it's just a matter of time before the sheep scatter.

Then Jesus said to them, "All of you will be made to stumble because of Me this night, for it is written: 'I will strike the Shepherd, And the sheep of the flock will be scattered.'" Matthew 26:31.

We decided not to share the bigger picture with the leaders. We told them that my husband's job was transferring him to Jordan, to oversee a project and we weren't sure how long we'd be away for, but we'd return. That was the truth in part, because his company had offered him something with the company's subsidiary, operating in Jordan and Egypt. They had also promised to continue fighting the government to reverse their decision. But it was the truth. That made it easy for him to communicate this in a way to ensure there was no fear in the camp.

Prior to our announcement, my husband decided to do a Holy Ghost power pack revival that shook the whole church and the land. He poured out his all. The Holy Spirit took control of him, miracles happened, lives were changed, many souls came to Christ, captives were set free. Apart from 2011 revival, we'd not heard that power pack revival. Over three days, he spoke to the church in parables about our imminent departure. He cried as he ministered to the church. He mentioned some things that those who were closely connected to him in spirit, were able to sense that something was not quite right. Of those whose eyes of the spirit were not enlightened, they didn't sense a thing. But it was a powerful revival. I also had to hold back my emotions. I couldn't break down in front of anyone. I couldn't tell anyone and dealt with the pain silently. You heal quickly when you share your pain, it takes a lot longer to heal when you are alone.

My husband called for a meeting with the Pastors and the elders of the church. We went to the meeting to announce our departure plans and to talk about the way forward. Some did not take the news well, some took it in faith, with the belief that we would return. To my surprise, the primary concern of others revolved around who would take our place as the powers of the church. I was shocked to actually hear that a close friend and member was more interested in becoming the First Lady of the church. There was no sign of sadness, or loss. She saw my vacant position as something to contest for, but for the wrong reasons. She saw it as a position where she could be in control of women, while being in a position of respect to others. What she hadn't realised was that I never held control over anybody. I was a servant to all. She had no idea what I'd had to deal with physically, spiritually and emotionally. She had no idea of the challenges the First Lady faced. If you are a First Lady, a Pastor's wife, or spouse to someone in a position of influence, and you are reading this book, you will understand what I'm talking about. If you are a Pastor's child, you will also have an idea of what your mother had to deal with. This woman only saw the glamorous element, she didn't know about the pain that came with the position. Hearing this woman's thoughts was like being cut again. "Church folks"! Mmmm! She irritated me in an instant. I never believed she'd behave in this manner. As a matter of fact, I had expected more sympathy from her than from anyone else, as our families were very close, our children were friends, and her husband was the closest associate to my husband. It seemed as though she'd been vying for the position of the First Lady all along! Since our announcement, she'd made her desire so obvious, people were beginning to think that her husband and herself deserved to be the next resident Pastors. I was broken. I mean, really broken. The kind of broken you become when someone, who you considered a good friend, one you relied on and trusted to support you in times of trouble, turned out to be interested in benefitting from your troubles. They saw your troubles as an opportunity for them to climb the ladder of recognition. A position they'd longed for all along. I felt so stupid to have trusted and loved this person and her family. I felt betrayed. It was like she'd put a dagger through me.

By now, my husband's name was already on the government's system as a wanted man. They treated us as though we were criminals. We weren't even able to sell our cars ...

Things turned very ugly, very quickly, to the extent that, if God wasn't on our side, there was a strong chance we'd end up leaving the country empty handed. We couldn't access our own personal funds because they'd frozen our bank accounts, and our savings outside the country were not easily accessible. No one was willing to help us, not even the church that we'd worked so hard to establish. We took so much risk and gave up our future for this church, but they wouldn't suggest any kind of help for us. This I couldn't, and still can't understand. It was becoming likely that we would have to leave without a send-off or goodbye service. The church administrator was afraid that members of the church would become weary of our departure and potentially create a setback for the church. It is true that we told the leaders we would be coming back, we just weren't sure when. It was normal to have a leaving do, even for regular people, regardless of whether they returned. It took one of our Pastors, who'd started the church with us, and her husband, to stand their ground and insist we be honoured. "Pastor Victor and Pastor Ola are the Founders of this church, they put their all into creating this church and taking it to where it is now. If it weren't for them, all of us would not have a place, a church, to worship in; a place we stand as leaders today. We must send them away in an appropriate manner." The Pastor and her husband pushed for us to be celebrated, otherwise we would have left as "nobody".

My husband had to make a decision on who to leave in charge while we were away. It was a tough decision for him to make. He prayed and prayed for guidance, but as our departure date neared, he had to make a decision fast.

Our last day in Saudi Arabia arrived. We had gone through so much at the hands of the locals;

we couldn't wait to leave the country. I just wanted to put all this behind me. We arrived with joy and were leaving in sadness. It was time to pretend that the past seven years of my life hadn't happened. It was time to focus on what God had in store for my family. I worried about how long it would take for my husband to find another job because he wasn't sure he was going to take the Jordan offer, what the community of our new rented accommodation, which our caretaker in England had helped secure, would be like. And the children? What would become of them? Life in Saudi Arabia was what they'd become accustomed to, especially the two younger boys. One had been born there, and the other one was only three when we migrated there. This would be the first time they'd be schooled in England. Would they settle in quickly and smoothly? Would our elder son, who was due to sit his GCSEs, actually be able to sit for these? My head was full of these thoughts and uncertainties. We said goodbye to Saudi Arabia and flew back to our base in the UK. We went straight to the apartment we'd rented for few days before our long-term rental accommodation was ready. I looked at my family and began to cry again. "Lord, you know what we don't. I do not understand all of this, but I know you do. I am convinced that, when you are done, I'm going to have every cause to praise and glorify you."

We finally moved into our new home. The neighbourhood was just what we wanted and we loved it. We spent some time looking at schools for our younger boys. God came with us and helped us choose the right one. However, our search for a school where our older son could take his exams was a dead end. We just couldn't find one. Every school we approached wouldn't accommodate him as it was too late for them to find a centre for him. He ended up repeating the year. But we still give God the praise, because it could have been worse. We could have still been locked up in that Saudi prison. That's what they'd done to a lot of the Christians there. The fact that God had intervened was the only reason they hadn't been able to touch us. God took us out safely. Something I will forever thank God for.

We eventually settled down and came to terms with the new environment God had brought us to. It was then that my husband got a call from his former boss, the CEO who'd stood by us and helped us leave safely. He called to ask if my husband would consider the offer in Jordan or Egypt. The salary offered was half of what he'd been earning, but he was eager to take it so he could take care of his family. He started work a month after we'd left Saudi Arabia. I'd only just resurfaced from the big ocean of pain of having to leave the monument behind, and now I had to be separated from my husband. "Lord, don't you think this is too much for one person to handle?" I complained. Another separation I hadn't factored into my plans. The reality was that if my husband didn't take up this offer, we would be financially challenged. So, I didn't really have much choice but to let him go.

I was now left alone to deal with my pain, left alone to take care of our children, and still be there when my husband needed me. But there was no one there for me. I know God was with me, and I could always depend on Him, but God wasn't a physical presence. I couldn't talk face-to-face with Him. I needed a shoulder to physically cry on. Everybody saw me as a strong person, one who could cope well when the storm of life hit. I knew how to manage my pain very well. Even if we slept in the same bed, you wouldn't have noticed my suffering. I'd been through so much in my life that I'd learnt to bottle things up. I wasn't really that strong, but I forced myself to appear strong. I did it for the sake of others and for myself.

Each time I went to church and saw how they were blooming, I bled. Every conversation I had with church people reminded me of my past experience, and I bled again.

Four weeks after we'd returned to the UK, I went to a conference to meet different Pastors and talk about their ministries; it made me bleed. As if my pain wasn't enough, the same woman who'd wanted the First Lady position, who'd basically ignored me and hadn't even come to the airport to see us off after my husband decided there would be no resident Pastor and no First Lady in our absence, was at the same conference. I had to allow the Holy Spirit to work its magic in me. I greeted her with an embrace, as though nothing had happened. I can tell you, that didn't come from me, it was the Holy Spirit. Two days into the conference, I walked into the auditorium. We had both been given special seats as the Pastor of this church had been to our church in Riyadh. I'd been invited to the conference before we left Saudi Arabia. I found this lady by the seats, she was talking to some people and I went over to greet the Pastors. I introduced myself to one of the South African Pastors, who I'd not met the night before. I stretched my hand out to her and introduced myself, told her I was here on a special assignment, and I mentioned the church I came from. Her response shocked me. She said, "Oh! Are you the ex-Pastor's wife?" I looked straight into the eyes of the woman who'd wanted to be the First Lady, the same Pastor my husband and I had ordained, and wished the ground would open up and swallow her. She literally turned red. She probably never realised the South African Pastor would tell me what she'd said to her. So I told the South African Pastor that I was not an ex-Pastors wife, that we were on an assignment and would return, because those were the words God had spoken to me in one of my dreams before we left. "Mopelola, you will do this again."

For the rest of that evening, that horrid friend of ours continued to lie, "I didn't tell that lady about your situation". So how else could she have known? We'd never met before, she couldn't know anything about my situation, how else would she have found out? That night another sword passed through me and my bleeding increased. It had not even been a month, but we were already a thing of the past. These are the people we left everything for. My husband left this friend's husband in-charge of the church, not because he was the best of all our Pastors, but because he was in a better position to call on others to do what they needed to do with few interruptions.

I returned home and started grieving. If it weren't for Jesus, I would have fallen into a serious depression, which could have lead anywhere imaginable in a situation like mine. I spent most of my time reading the bible. It was the only place I could draw strength from. I prayed like I'd never prayed before. I stopped watching our church service online, as it broke my heart each time I saw the people there. One day, I heard God say, "You've got to let go of this child that you have lost. If you can take your eyes off it and trust me, I will help heal your wound and you can have your life back." So I completely cut out that part of my life, the only thing I didn't stop was the daily devotional that I wrote for the church, and until this moment, the writing of this book. I will continue until God says otherwise. God allowed me to detox. He did some renovation. He worked particularly hard in the area of forgiveness. I have always believed that no one could do anything that I would not be able to forgive, because it was a gift in me, given by God. I didn't realise that there were different levels of offence, where some required a higher level of forgiveness. There was something else that had happened between my husband and the Pastor he'd left in charge at the church in Saudi Arabia. It had caused a large rift and is not something I'm going to talk about in this book, but it left me feeling completely hateful. One morning, I was praying and the Holy Spirit said to me, "You have not been praying for the leaders in your church as you used to do, especially this lady." "Lord, you are kidding me right". "No, I'm not," I heard Him say to my heart. "Father, you do realise that I'm not Jesus," I said. His response during my prayer time was, "If you want me to walk you through this pain, you're going to have to start praying for them, especially this lady." I was crushed by His words. It was so bad that, for two days, God and I didn't communicate. I didn't speak to Him; He didn't speak to me. For those two days, I refused to pray, didn't even read my bible … and this was one thing I hadn't stopped in a while. Even if it was just one line, I had to read my bible daily, otherwise I felt like I couldn't breathe. On the third day, I woke up unbelievably peaceful and began to pray for everyone who had something to do with my pain. The Holy Spirit took over from me and I began to shower blessings on them. With

God as my witness, that day, I prayed for so long that, by the time I was done, my clothes were soaked. I felt like I'd won the lottery when I got up from my knees. My week was filled with this unbelievable joy. I remember thanking God for bringing me back to me. I am naturally a joyful person. I like to make everyone around me feel good and I rarely got into a mood. Three weeks, and I was still filled with joy; the kind of joy only God could give. The following week, the Lord spoke to me again during my prayers. He told me to pick up the phone, call the lady and apologise to her. He told me to say I was sorry for all that had happened and that I wasn't to tell my husband, or anyone else about it. That's when I said, "Hold it right there, Lord. I didn't do anything to this person. Shouldn't she be the one saying sorry?" And then I reminded him about my pain, as if He didn't already know. His gentle voice spoke to my heart, "I know, my child. Remember Jesus, my son, didn't do anything wrong either. But remember what they did to him and how he overcame this through His obedience to me. It was to save you and the rest of the world." "Well, with no disrespect, God, I am not Jesus. I don't have to take what he took." So he asked me, "What would Jesus do if it had been him who'd been treated the way you've been treated?" "I don't know," I lied, forgetting that He was the all knowing God. "Lord, how are you going to make me do that? Isn't praying for her good enough. I'm happy praying for her, but to pick up the phone and call her and say

I'm sorry? For what?" I ended my conversation with God and went about my daily business. Towards the evening, I felt like I'd disrespected my Heavenly Father, so I picked up my iPad and sent her a message. Exactly what God had asked me to do and copied in my husband. It was easier for me that way. Then I left it alone. To my surprise, the lady wrote back. With a huge sense of relief, she apologised to me too. I couldn't stop crying. I cannot describe the joy that flooded through my heart. I turned to God in my night prayer. I was like a little child who couldn't wait to tell her dad all about her achievement. Two days later, I called her on FaceTime and we spoke like nothing had ever happened between us. This is the power of God in man. As I write about this experience, I feel no bitterness towards her, or anyone else I'd held things against.

Now, let me relate to those who have gone through or are going through a pain similar to mine. Perhaps your marriage was your investment and someone took it from you; perhaps it was your business that was taken away from you; or the children you did everything for so they could become somebody, and now that they were successful, they want little to do with you, or simply don't care about you. Whatever the cause of your pain, firstly, I want you to know that there is a light at the end of this tunnel of pain. Secondly, you need to realise that it's not necessarily something that you've done that made them treat you this way. If God had no involvement, it wouldn't have happened. Thirdly, you must know that your disappointment is for a new appointment, your displacement is for a new placement. When God closes one door, He always opens a bigger door. Always remember that you cannot go through your pain without God holding your hand. It's important not to walk away from Him. You need Him, so hold onto Him. You must allow God to work with you through your pain, He does it better than anyone. You must also be willing to work with Him, because He will not do anything without your willingness, surrender and trust in Him. He will see you through your time of pain. Lastly, you must allow God to help you with forgiveness. If Jesus hadn't forgiven mankind, there would have been no salvation. He forgave your sins before you were created, that's our belief, and if He went through all of that for your sins to be forgiven, you have no excuse not to forgive as well. Don't allow mere men to take your eternity from you. Don't lose your place in heaven because you are unable to forgive. Although your sorrow may last for a night, joy will come in the morning. All things will come together for the better, and in the end, you will laugh and glorify God. If God hadn't made us leave Riyadh, you wouldn't be reading this book. Why? Because I wouldn't have had my experience to write about, then help you through your pain. Though we don't have a million pounds in our account right now, I know it's coming. God has restored many things that were lacking in our marriage and in our journey of faith. Unfortunately, these are things I cannot write about in this book. You have a life to live and the opportunity to make an impact in the world around you.

Chapter Seven
Don't Give in to the Guilt

"Watch and pray, that you don't enter into temptation. The spirit indeed is willing, but the flesh is weak." ... Matthew 26:41

On three occasions, Jesus visited his friends, the ones who'd journeyed with him to the place of press, but couldn't stay. Their eyes were suffering from lack of sleep, they just couldn't keep them open. I know the feeling, when all you need is sleep, nothing matters. As a mother, I know what it feels like to hear the cry of your baby in the middle of the night while in a deep sleep. It's a choice between feeding the baby properly or shutting your eyes in sleep and letting the baby fumble with a pacifier. The pacifier doesn't come close to the satisfaction gained from a proper breastfeed. There were many times I woke up feeling guilty about forfeiting the baby's feed for uncontrollable sleep.

Being there for someone is the least that is expected when we are considered friends. It really is the minimum a friend could do. Our bond is soothing when all is smooth. Our relationship is pleasant when all is pleasurable and peaceful, but how long can a friend remain by your side when things start to fall apart? How much can you achieve when the power of sleep overcomes you in your midnight hour, when you needed to watch in prayer for someone? To what extent can I count on you when you're the only person I expect to be by my side? These expectations have set the foundation for the blame game that fuels the sense of guilt during separation. Not only do we blame people for not being there for us, we play on their emotions until they drown in guilt. Jesus was quite aware that the disciples would wake up with the awareness of his expectations of them as friends when they were at the press. It was clear that, someday, they'd realise they hadn't been able to keep their eyes open to watch over him in his darkest hour. Jesus knew that they would start to feel the guilt when they looked back on what they'd done. That was why he'd warned them to not fall into the trap of guilt. You can never give what you don't have. If God never positioned you to be my help, if God never gave you the grace to know what, when, and how to do it, you wouldn't have the capacity to deliver to my expectations. I'd never realised this before, despite everything I'd been through, but as God guides me through the healing process, I am beginning to appreciate the spiritual understanding of the dynamics behind relationships. This has enabled me to forgive myself and others.

Relationships are bound by time, level and purpose. I learnt this from my husband as I observed his dealings in situations and with people. Despite the lack of physical or emotional support during our crisis in Saudi Arabia, even from people we considered our associates or those we looked up to as spiritual fathers, it did not change who he was. His dealings and level of respect for them remained unchanged. It sometimes bothered me that he continued to demonstrate his love and respect for them, especially as I considered them traitors and users. Whenever I mentioned my thoughts on this, he simply told me that his relationship with them was time bound, level bound and purpose bound. He always told me that friends would only be friends until they'd served their purpose in life. They could only give what was within their capacity, something that could end when their time was up. Without a decent comprehension of this, you will find it difficult to find satisfaction in their actions, or you may feel guilty for what you've done.

Forgiveness can only come from understanding. We find it difficult to forgive people when we experience separation because of the limitations in our understanding of the truth and the limited view of the full picture surrounding the situation.

We hold people accountable for things that were originally planned by God, and in most instances we hold ourselves accountable for failed marriages, friendships, or family disconnections. That is not good for our destiny, neither is the pain worth it.

Judas never forgave himself. He was destroyed by the guilt of betraying Jesus. It is true that his desires and passion for money clouded his judgment. However, it was his destiny to betray Jesus. His self-guilt pushed him to suicide, he never gave himself the opportunity to forgive himself. Jesus forgave him because of his ability to understand. For every journey we make in life, there are people God has placed throughout, for a specific time and reason. Sometimes they bring good, sometimes they bring pain, but please understand that God has a perfect reason for placing them in our life.

The traditional marriage solemnisation includes the phrase "till death do us part", which means a marriage does not last forever, it is time bound. Similarly, relationships can be segmented into different levels. There are people you call close friends, best friends and other variations of friendship, but their position in your life determines the space you give them in your heart. For example, certain rooms in your house will only accommodate certain friends, depending on the level of friendship you have with them. There are some friends who we invite into our living rooms. There are some who we allow into the kitchen, and another level of friends may be invited to your bedroom. You know who they are, and what they represent. You know who you can trust with your secrets and who would watch your back if anything went wrong. You know which ones are there for their own benefit, you also know those who are friendly due to who you know. Whatever the reason, someone is in your life. When their purpose has been fulfilled, the time for separation will set in.

Now, when I look back at why I'd been so bruised and had bled so much from the experiences we encountered in Saudi Arabia, I realise it had nothing to do with anything but where I held those people in my heart. Time helped me. When I needed them the most, they did not stand by me. If I had known what I know now, I wouldn't have bled so much and I could have overcome the pain sooner.

Look at Peter, who Jesus called the "Rock". He spent a lot of time with Jesus, and Jesus considered him a confidant. But Peter betrayed Jesus three times. Yes, what Judas did was horrible, but I don't see the difference between Judas's actions and Peter's. As far as I'm concerned, they were both disloyal. I believe Peter's betrayal was more painful because he was closer to Jesus.

Those who are closest, funnily enough, are the ones who are capable of hurting you the most.

How did Jesus get past that? I think it was because of his understanding; the understanding of Peter's limitations and what the journey of separation would entail.

"And the Lord said, 'Simon, Simon! Indeed, Satan has asked for you, that he may sift you as wheat. But I have prayed for you; that your faith should not fail; and when you have returned to Me, strengthen your brethren.'" Luke 22:31-32.

I can only imagine the emotional turmoil Peter went through when he realised what he'd done to his master and friend ... to the one who'd shown Peter the way of life, the one who'd held Peter's as a rock, upon which the church would be built ... When loyalty was due, Peter denied this to Jesus. That was awful and painful in itself, but Peter had to move past this so he could position himself for the future the master was going to leave behind.

Although Jesus had come to eliminate our sins, he represented love and was always forgiving. But these weren't the reasons Jesus forgave Peter.

Jesus did not harbour any hard feelings because the future of the church was at stake. His understanding was evident even before Peter's disloyalty. If you make room for what God has planned, and prevent your emotions from overruling you, it will be easier to clearly see why things happen when they happen, as well as their underlying cause. This understanding has helped me a lot and has given me a great deal of relief in times of hardship.

Purpose determines power. It determines how you relate to anything and everything, including relationships. The bond between a father and daughter, mother and son, siblings, colleagues, fellow church members, and husband and wife, are all purpose driven. It doesn't have to last for eternity, but their place in your journey will fulfil its purpose. Judas was destined to journey with Jesus to Calvary. Peter's purpose was to allow for continuity and to enable establishment of Jesus's words. Would you have chosen someone like Peter, someone who'd prevented you, not once but three times, from the opportunity to lead the church you'd conceived and created with your own blood and sweat? This is the mystery behind purpose. We could ruin our futures by letting negative experiences linger without forgiveness. It's best to overcome the guilt and step into your new purpose. If you can't change it, that simply means God ordained it. Remember, people will come and go, but the words of God remain unchanged and abides forever.

It has often happened that we are unable to forgive ourselves for something someone has blamed us of doing, believing that we failed them somehow. Many Christians today are crippled by their inability to grasp God's forgiveness and they live their lives feeling guilty. They are unable to comprehend why God would forgive someone like them. Their enemy led them to believe they didn't deserve God's unmerited favour, leaving them weighed down with guilt, living in the past rather than the future. It's time for you to break away from those past failings and embrace God's forgiveness.

It's time to let go of those who have hurt and disappointed you, of those who weren't there when you needed them. These people simply didn't have the power to be there for you. They may have wanted to, but couldn't because that's how God set out your destiny. We have not been given everything, we've been given what we need to do. Going beyond your God given capacity could lead to disappointment. We must always try our best and sometimes stretch beyond our comfort zone, but if our best fails, it means God wants it that way.

Jesus, in his darkest hour, placed expectations on his close friends, hoping they would watch out for him while he prayed, but they couldn't. Why? Because he was asking them to do something they didn't have power to do. He was asking them for something they didn't possess. Jesus eventually understood that his friends were not meant to join him in his next steps. So, instead of being angry with them, he was more concerned about the guilt they'd encounter when they realised they'd been unable to help Jesus when he needed them the most. Your Gethsemane is your place, where you are alone with God. Sometimes God needs you to work with him in isolation. In this instance, he will separate you from people and places, people you love dearly, and your beloved job or business. This is the moment when it seems as though the whole world is against you, it's you against them … wrong. It is you and God. When God places you in this situation, where your friend needs you, but you can't follow, don't drown in the guilt — guilt is nothing more than a temptation.

In 1987, my mother was very ill. Back then, my mother didn't have access to a telephone, so she couldn't call her children to inform us that she was ill. She also lived hundreds of miles away from us and had to wait until someone travelled to the city where my brother and I were living. It was a week before the message got to us. Two days later, I left on my own to be with her. My brother was very busy at work and asked me to go and stay with her until she was better. He also gave me some money for the travel fare. On arriving at the bus station, I discovered that the fare amount wasn't enough to take me to the village. I know my brother had given me the last of his money, so going back to him was not an option. I thought about what to do next.

I then remembered my boyfriend's mother, who lived in another city not too far from my mother. I had enough money to get to her. She would be able to help me get to my village. That became my plan. It was a little late in the evening when I arrived at her place. She persuaded me to stay the night as it wasn't safe for a young girl like myself to travel alone to my mother's part of town. I took her advice and stayed in her house overnight. I woke up as early as possible, starting the rest of my journey in the early hours of the day. I was looking forward to seeing my mother.

I had a vast number of thoughts running through my head, about what I'd find my mother doing when I got home. They were thoughts of everything I could imagine. I couldn't help but visualise her reading her bible, or perhaps not. Maybe she was doing some cleaning, she couldn't stand any kind of dirt in the house. I was actually looking forward to her cooking as I'd not eaten her food for six months, I missed it. My imagination captured everything apart from death.

As I approached the gate to our house, I couldn't see my mother, but there were some women standing outside. Going through the gate, I saw my mother's younger sister sitting on the floor crying. I quickly ran to her and asked why she was crying. At first I thought it was my grandmother, as she lived with my mother. So I asked, "Is grandma dead?" She shook her head and said, "It's my sister, your mother. She died eight o'clock this morning." I sat on the floor with her and we both cried together. My mother died two hours before my arrival. If I had arrived the night before, I would have seen her alive.

From that moment onwards, I blamed myself for not trying hard enough to be there before she passed away. I carried the guilt of letting my mother down when she needed me the most. It was bad when my own brother, who'd provided the cost of the transportation, wouldn't believe my story. To this day, some of my family still hold that against me. As though my presence would have stopped her from dying. I couldn't forgive myself for what was beyond my power. I carried the guilt on my shoulders for twenty-seven years, until God introduced my spiritual understanding on how I wasn't meant to be there as my mother was dying. I did not have the ability to get to her before she died, though I tried my best to do so. I simply didn't have the power or privilege to meet the expectation that was set on me.

Although she was my mother, it didn't change the fact that I didn't possess what it took to be there when she needed me the most. However, it was impossible for me to give what I didn't have. It has taken me twenty-seven years to forgive myself and break free of the guilt I'd carried all these long years. You need to accept that it was not your fault that what actually happened, happened. You were not meant to understand that level of expectation. You simply weren't given the power for that. Stop blaming yourself for what was written before the foundation of the world. What is written, is written. No one can change that. I know your son killed himself, I know your daughter took her own life, I know your baby died under your watch, I know you lost that job your family depended on, I know you walked out on that marriage because you'd had enough and your children blamed you or made you feel guilty for leaving their father … I know any of that could have happened. That's why I'm here, to represent the voice of God in your head. It is time to stop blaming yourself for whatever it is that happened to you in the past.

It is time to free yourself of the guilt of failing your siblings, friends, parents, children, colleagues, church families. It is time to receive God's forgiveness and move on with your life. It is time to stop living with the guilt of what happened in the past. It is called the past because it no longer exists. It doesn't have the right to feature in the present or future. It wasn't your fault — **The Spirit was willing but the flesh is weak** — don't fall into the temptation of running away from your family or those that you have let down. Don't give into the temptation of not forgiving yourself. That was what Jesus was trying to tell Peter, James and John. **The Spirit was willing but the flesh is weak** — Jesus said, "I know you want to help me, but you don't have the capacity to come with me to the next level of my journey."

Perhaps there was a time when you expected someone to stand by you, but they didn't. God took you through anyway — do you ever, even for a moment, think that perhaps their spirit was willing, but their flesh couldn't. It is not about you and them, it is about you and God ... you were disassociated from them so you could move onto the next level of your assignment. If you can just stay with God and stop looking for human forgiveness and affirmation, you will find yourself in a place of victory. Perhaps you are still upset with the person who was with you, but didn't stay ... look unto Jesus. Maybe you thought that if you came back, they'd be there, waiting for you, but they were gone. Don't worry — look unto Jesus

Perhaps you are suffering with the guilt of not being there for someone when they needed you the most. This is the devil tempting you with the barrier that will keep you from moving forward, and from succeeding when you want to help somebody.

The enemy, for many years, kept me bound in guilt. He made me believe that I was no good to anyone. "You cannot be trusted, or depended on. You are useless to yourself and to the human race," he whispered in my ears. Some people would find this concept hard to believe. I believed the words spoken to me. For many years, I justified the things I was doing to people, things that may not have had anything to do with them. I tried to prove myself to people in order to gain their acceptance and approval. Don't waste precious time in your life believing the enemy. If God is not condemning you, why are you condemning yourself? Break free of it while you still can.

God's desire and plan doesn't include watching you wallow in guilt and the inability to forgive. Guilt and being unable to forgive will act as a blindfold, keeping you in the dark. It also takes away your joy. One of the things I always say to people whenever I have the privilege to counsel them, is that forgiveness is for you, not for the other person. When you forgive, you forgive for yourself. Not forgiving people equates to them still holding onto the power they had over you when they were offensive. If you do not forgive, you are giving them the power to affect your life. Their control over your life remains, even in their physical absence. They live inside of you. You get bitter and angry whenever they are mentioned. It brings back memories of what they did to you, and opens up your pain again. They've probably moved on from when they hurt you. By not forgiving them, you're inviting your pain to stay. They have moved on, but you're still wallowing in pain. You've got to press the delete button by forgiving them.

The pain of separation is mostly embedded in the inability to forgive, and the feeling of guilt. The man is gone, the woman is gone, he is not coming back, she is not coming back, so spruce yourself up and move on. It is a new day. Let go of the pain that you have carried for far too long. Embrace God's forgiveness, forgive others and yourself, then watch the joy flood back into your heart. Watch your life change. Watch God deliver the right man or woman, who will love and care for you the way God does. God will do the impossible in your life. He is the only one who can fix that which is broken. He loves you more than you can imagine. Allow the peace of God in your heart. Let God take you to places where you never thought you could go. *"For as many as are led by the spirit of God, these are the sons of God Romans"* 8:14.

Chapter Eight

The Place of Confusion, Confrontation and Conformity

And he went forward a little, and fell on his face, and prayed, saying, My Father, if it be possible, let this cup pass away from me: nevertheless, not as I will, but as thou wilt ... Matthew 26:39 ASV

To stop the haemorrhaging caused by separation, as with any other kind of bleeding, it needs to be done in phases. It doesn't matter what you are separated from, profuse bleeding sets in straightaway. The bleeding drains you and aggravates the pain in all aspects of your life. The wound starts to trigger the offensive, which is manifested in your attitude, emotional disposition and behaviour. Your children start to feel isolated and sometimes neglected. Your friends are kept away.

It is worse when you cannot rebound quickly. It would have been easier if you'd lost your man to another woman. You could easily replace the physical element of your man soon enough, even just for the heck of it. But when the business you'd spent your life building suddenly disappears or your hard earned savings are swallowed by a scam, or the child you just kissed with the promise of "see you later" is wrapped in the coroner's body bag an hour later, shot dead by a drive-by shooter on his way to school, you need various stages to stop this form of internal bleeding.

The best way to overcome the pain of separation is to understand the three stages that you will go through before you reach the place of permanent victory and healing. In my own opinion, the three stages of recovery are confusion, confrontation and conformation.

The Confusion Stage

Confusion? Yes, confusion. The stage where you confuse blood with body fluid, sweat or even red dye. The stage where you sit in denial, which then forces you into a place of false hope. When the unexpected strikes, how do you deal with it?

At one point or another in our lives, we will have to deal with unexpected and prodigious circumstances. How we manage the situation individually is based on our ability to accept that we have a situation and refrain from denial.

The confusion stage is the state of being bewildered or unclear about something in one's mind. It is the stage where uncertainty, perplexity, and disorientation prevails. Confusion presents us with different options or solutions, but the first choice we often make is denial. To be in denial means refusing to accept or believe that what happened actually happened. You refuse to acknowledge that it's really happening, and behave in ways that may seem bizarre to others. For example, in the case of a mother losing her only daughter in a car accident, the mother will be in a state of shock for days, if not weeks. Then she will move to the state of confusion, which could then escalate to denial. Denial would then take her to a place of false hope.

The pain of losing someone you love dearly will numb you. You know this person is gone and will never come back, but you can't accept this fact. You hope it's just a horrible nightmare that will end when you wake up, and everything will be normal. Deep inside, you know this isn't a nightmare, it's reality. Not accepting the situation won't change things for the better, it will only make things worse. When we go through the pain of losing our loved ones, either from death or from separation, it's normal to imagine they are still there, because it's more convenient to convince ourselves that nothing has happened. We are confused, can't come to terms with our loss, and can't comprehend it. But the fact is staring us in the face. Brushing it under the carpet will not make things better.

To illustrate this point, there is a story of a woman and her husband, who loved each other and had a wonderful family. One morning, they both woke up in the same bed and made their separate ways to work after dropping the children off at school.

About midday, the wife was having lunch in the staff room. She sat down to listen to the news. As she turned on the television, the first news story she heard was of a bomb that had gone off at the train station her husband caught a connecting train to work that morning. She ran out of the staff room to get her phone and called her husband to make sure he was OK. To her surprise, a female police officer answered. Of course, when you call your husband on his cell phone and a woman answers, your first move would be to check you've dialled the right number. If it was the right number, your next question is, "Who are you and why are you answering my husband's phone?" That would generally be the normal response to a woman answering your husband's phone. But the fear of bad news had crowded her mind and she didn't do what you and I would probably do.

The first thing she said when the dial tone indicated the call had been connected was, "Honey, are you okay?" Of course, the female police officer saw "WIFE" on the caller ID. "I am so sorry madam. Your husband is in a critical condition because of an explosion that occurred this morning. We are not sure if he is going to make it but the doctors are trying everything possible to keep him alive." She screamed, and asked for the name of the hospital they'd taken her husband to. She got into a taxi and went straight to the hospital; her husband died five minutes before she got there.

Oh! Her world crumbled. The news about her husband's death numbed her completely. She couldn't talk. She was taken to a room where one of the hospital counsellors sat and spoke with her. She didn't hear a word the counsellor said, all she did was stare at the walls of the room. Finally, she got up, went to her car and drove home. As she opened the door, she called out, "Honey, I'm home." No response. She started making dinner for the family around two o'clock in the afternoon, then went to pick up the children from school. She didn't tell the children that their father was dead. Back at home, she sat down with the children to watch television. At one point, one of the children flipped to the news channel. Their father's death had made the headlines, which also showed their mother arriving at the hospital and her reaction to being told her husband was dead. The children, of course, were shocked, crying from the grief of losing their father.

The oldest child sensed that something was not quite right with their mother. She was naturally an emotional person, one who cried whenever she watched an emotional movie. But their mum was not crying. Something was not right, the older child thought. It was as though their mother was watching the same news but not actually hearing the words. A few minutes later, the mum went to the front door, "Honey, is that you?" and opened the door, but there was no one there. "Oh, I thought it was your father," she said to her daughter. Her daughters were crying, but she hadn't noticed their grief. The mother then went into their bedroom and started making the bed and folding clothes she had washed the previous day. When she came back downstairs, she asked the children whether their dad was back yet? "Mum, dad died this morning in a bomb accident." "Stop that nonsense and stop wishing your father evil. He is not dead, he went to work and he will be right back." She'd lost her mind. The family got together and arranged for the funeral and buried him.

However, this woman had failed to accept her husband's death, she couldn't believe he was gone and still hoped he would just walk in through the door. She went to the extent of putting his food on the table every single day for three years. She said, "Good morning, honey" every morning when she woke up. She even went to the train station as though she was dropping her husband off. Her reaction to the pain of her loss may seem bizarre to many, but that just tells you how deeply she was cut. It tells you how badly she was bleeding. It expresses the impact her loss had had on her. The quickest way out for her had been to stay in a state of denial and false hope; a state that kept her bound in her pain for three years. If it took her three years to accept her pain of separation, you can only imagine the length of time it would take for her to heal. You can only hope that a person like her would eventually move on in life without their pain.

Your pain of separation may not be death. It may be your relationship with a spouse. It may be not getting into the university you dreamt of. It may be you were fired from the job you worked hard for, and the loss of the position and friendships you had built there. It may be that your husband, who you'd been married to for years, leaves you for another man. Whatever your situation is, you've got to understand that the situation is there. You've got to accept it, not pretend that it's not happening or didn't happen.

King Saul in the bible is another example of someone who was in a state of confusion, which opened up a space for him in the seat of denial, setting him up for false hope, making him do some stupid things, and eventually losing his mind. King Saul was anointed and proclaimed as the King of

Israel (1 Samuel 10). In 1 Samuel chapter 13, he made an unlawful sacrifice unto God that made prophet Samuel proclaim God's judgment on him and his entire generation.

"And Samuel said to Saul, 'You have done foolishly. You have not kept the commandment of the LORD your God, which He commanded you. For now, the LORD would have established your kingdom over Israel forever. But now your kingdom shall not continue. The LORD has sought for Himself a man after His own heart, and the LORD has commanded him to be commander over His people, because you have not kept what the LORD commanded you.'" I Samuel 13:13-14 NKJV.

Saul just couldn't understand, or perhaps he just refused to accept the fact that his kingdom was not going to continue because he'd made the wrong sacrifice unto the Lord. Perhaps he thought it wouldn't make much of a difference whether he made the sacrifice or not. He just couldn't accept the fact that God had chosen him as King of Israel and then, that same God then rejected him and appointed someone else to rule over Israel. It was too much for him to handle or comprehend. He had been the chosen king and denunciating him was not something he accepted, so he sat on the seat of denial for a very long time. Though, he ruled over Israel as King, it did not change the fact that God had already ended the relationship between Himself and

Saul. Years later, God dissolved the Israeli kingdom. Saul made another error, one that made God regret He'd appointed Saul as king in the first place. It led to God re-affirming His decision to denounce Saul and remove him as king over the people of Israel. And as Samuel turned around to go away, Saul seized the edge of his robe, and it tore. So Samuel said to him, "The Lord hath rent the kingdom of Israel from thee this day, and hath given it to a neighbour of thine, that is better than thou". I Samuel 15:27-29 NKJV.

The story of Saul was not a story of a pain resulting from the loss of a spouse or children. It was the pain of losing a position, and the power and glamour that came with it. It would have been better for him to not have been king, than a king who'd led the people of Israel for quite some time, especially as he'd been the first King of Israel. It sounded like an impossible feat to him. The pain of losing his position, along with the associated powers slipping out of his hands, was not something his mind wanted to process. As he'd failed to accept this, he couldn't address it. Unable to address it meant he couldn't surrender to God's proclamation, which meant he lost everything, including his mind.

I was also in a state of confusion when God initiated our departure from the church in Saudi Arabia, the same church he'd used us to build. I just couldn't understand it, couldn't comprehend that I'd have to leave the church my womb had carried and given birth to. The church that we'd put so much effort into. Then, just when it was time to take it to the next level, bam, it was time to move on. Not our will, but "His will". I am not going to pretend it was a piece of cake for me to overcome the pain of separating from the church. I was in so much denial, I even believed the Minister when he said, "I just want him out now and he can come back after a year," referring to my husband. Deep down in my heart, I knew he was lying, I knew he couldn't be trusted. A part of me also knew that he was just saying this to get rid of us. It was unlikely we'd return to Saudi Arabia, unless God had another plan. Another part of me hoped we'd return soon. I just didn't allow myself to see the fact that God had sent us there for time and a reason. He was setting us up for our next assignment.

The longer you deny your loss, the longer it will take to heal your pain. The pain of loss is like a cut in the body. If you let it bleed, it will never clot, and if it doesn't clot, the bleeding won't stop, and your wound won't heal.

The Confrontation Stage

One of the Oxford Dictionary definitions of the word confrontation is "the technique used in group therapy, as in encounter groups, in which one is forced to recognise your shortcomings and their possible consequences". It is the point of showdown and affray — bringing two opposing forces into alignment. Sometimes we look or feel invincible when we are in a position where we have to show strength at our weakest moment. It is easy for us to not confront our weaknesses, and seek support instead. We are likely to continue in pain, bleeding on the inside, while help eludes us.

How many times have we come to terms with our separations, then shied away from reaching the point where we publicly accept that we are in pain? Jesus, the son of God, the Lord of the waves, the one all servants looked up to, even in the face of the fiercest storm, can turn to these disciples and openly declare. *"Then he said to them, 'My soul is overwhelmed with sorrow to the point of death'"* ... Matthew 26:38.

When the master is able to confront his weaknesses, it opens the doors to the healing process.

If you cannot acknowledge your pain with fellow man, you may not be able to acknowledge it with God either. It exists where there's only yourself and no one else. It's important to feel free to be able to talk to the people God has surrounded you with. They can hold your hand while you journey to the place of recovery. I see you saying, "Oh no! I'm not telling my business to anyone." I know some people have put your business out there before, when you confided in them, but you cannot let that be a barrier. You've got to open your heart to someone who can relate to your pain, someone who has experienced something similar themselves. It's not a place where you make excuses for the way you've handled your emotions. It's not a platform for either condemning or blaming yourself. You need to see it as a complete platform for healing purposes, which can only manifest itself if you confront it through prayers and your belief in God. Confronting your weakness prepares you for surrendering to God

As Jesus was separated from one level on his journey to the next level of his assignment, he was laden with emotions, fear and agony. He was suffering from serious inner pain and had no choice but to share it with his three friends. Even the creator stripped himself naked in the presence of the created. This is Jesus, the son of God, the eternal rock of ages, the king of the storm … now saying to his confidants, "My soul is sorrowful, even unto death …" You would have thought that Jesus had the ability to deal with problems himself, without having to pour his sorrowful heart out to these three — but that was the place of his confrontation … *Unless you confront your weaknesses, you will not command your strength.*

I know it's easy to bottle things up when the unexpected happens. For some, it is a way out of dealing with their pain. However, bottling up problems can be emotionally draining. Being pretentious and covering up your weaknesses and fear will only diminish your strength. As good as it sounds, it's not the best way to handle the pain of separation. It's definitely not the way God intended for you to deal with it. Jesus is a good example, and we need to be able to emulate him. Don't make it seem like you are the first, or the last, to experience such humiliation and separation. Far from it, your pain is definitely nothing to be ashamed of — you can be yourself.

Jesus, did not care whether his friends mocked him for having a weakness despite being the messiah. Instead he opened up to them. Though, at first, it seemed as though he couldn't comprehend why the people he called friends couldn't feel his pain, but he gently walked himself through the process. He wasn't blaming them for his problems, nor did he fail to accept that there was a problem.

In today's world, we raise our boys to not show emotions. It is generally assumed that boys who show their emotions are considered as being weak. "Big boys don't cry," is a phrase my husband uses a lot to encourage our youngest boy to bear pain. Big boys are taught to hold back their pain. I don't believe in all that. I don't think we are helping our boys to understand that it is OK to grieve and outwardly express their fears and emotions when they are faced with situations.

Even God expects us to show emotions, so why are we teaching our boys to hide their emotions?

Yes, we expect our boys to be tough and strong. Expressing your pain doesn't make you weak. It actually helps them develop into greater men. Great men are the ones who are able to express their emotions. If they cannot express their emotions to fellow man, how are they then expected to break down before their maker and surrender all. I believe that's one of the fundamental reasons why more women attend church nowadays. Perhaps men have been led to believe that church is only for women as they are the only gender that is free to express their natural emotions. Even when men do come to church, it's tough for them to come to the altar as they don't want to be seen as being soft.

A few years back, our first son, who lived and went to school in the US, came home for a vacation. Two weeks after his return, we travelled to Canada, for about four weeks. As our holiday came to an end, he had to go back to the US, and we had to go back to the UK. We all started getting emotional about this imminent separation. Two days before our departure, our eldest son and his siblings, along with the children of the family we were visiting, began teasing each other about how the following day would be one of tears for everybody. I expected every one of them to be emotional one way or the other, because emotion is part of our soul. Children often exaggerate things when they want to make a point. So they decided to tease our second son, also a naturally emotional person. He knew this about himself and told his older brother, he'd be upset when he saw all of us going one way and him another, alone. So the children had placed bets on what our first son said and I didn't know. Our final day arrived and our oldest son left in the morning, we left in the evening. As we went to see our son off at the airport, his siblings were all crying and saying their goodbyes. To my surprise, he was pacifying them, telling them not to cry and kept his cool. I took him to the airport and checked him in. He gave me a big hug and kissed me goodbye. As a mother, I couldn't hold back my tears and started crying. He held me tight while I cried. He didn't say a word and shed no tears himself. When he was about to board the plane, we separated, but he continued waving to me until the last moment. I cried until I got back to my other children, which took forty-five minutes of driving. As soon as I opened the door, they rushed over to me. Surprisingly, their first question was about whether their older brother had cried. I couldn't understand why they were particularly interested in his emotional state, and asked them. "We made a bet the other night that he would cry when you took him to the airport and he said he was not going to cry." I was furious with them for doing that to their brother. They'd deprived my boy of his freedom to express his emotions. Not only that, but they'd pushed him into behaving unnaturally. Though our son had not cried openly at the airport, I knew he was crying on the inside. I knew this from how he hugged me, how he couldn't stop waving, he didn't need to openly express the pain of his separation from the rest of the family at the time.

Your tears of pain are your truth to power.

I don't know what your story is, but my advice to you is that you don't have to suffer in silence. It's also important not to let anyone prevent you from grieving your own way. It's your right to confront your fears, your anxiety, your concerns, or whatever it is that will help you out of that ocean of bleeding, so just do it. No one else is experiencing what you are, they don't necessarily have an understanding of the amount of pain you are in. If you can't feel my pain, you will not know my purpose.

It's your life, it's your pain, and it's your decision; handle it your own way. Don't worry about what others say, they are entitled to their opinions, but their opinions should not affect what is inside you. Gather your strength today, and encourage yourself to take that step towards healing and get your life back.

The Stage of Conformity

Regardless of whether you are a believer or not, one thing it's important to be aware of, and not argue against, is that there will always be a point where you realise that you have not let go. It's not that you haven't done your best and you're giving up, it's just that when you get to this point, you just know that you have to let what's happening take its course. As a believer, I call it the point of surrender. You can call it the point where nature takes its course alternatively. Whatever you call this point, it is the point of complete solace. It feels good when something you've worked hard to eliminate, actually goes away. But if you don't conform, you will be crushed eventually.

The point of conformity, where you are able to relieve yourself of the pain of separation, is when you accept the perfect will of God. He has everything already worked out, you just aren't aware of it. The place of conformity is not a place of pleasure. It is where the pain peaks. It's also the point that is pivotal to your future, where you start to see things more clearly and think more logically.

All your emotions start to drop away and reality starts to set in.

Look at Jesus and his powerful saying while he experienced the last horrendous pain of separation … *"My Father, if it be possible, let this cup pass away from me: nevertheless, not as I will, but as thou wilt …"* Matthew 26:39 ASV.

The level of internal conflict this man was dealing was only resolved by reaching the point of conformity with the Father's will.

"I don't want to let go of this domain. It's not my will, but your will. I don't want to let go of this church, it's not my will, but your will." The more

I confessed this during my pain, the better I felt in spirit while I was drowning in the pain of loss, having lost the domain I'd laboured for.

Try not to cover a wound and bandage the sore. Leave it open and let the fresh air of God's Spirit blow on it. Don't try to be overly religious either. By reaching a point where you say, "Well, I will let go because God is paying me back for my sins" or you look to other forms of medication to sedate yourself to establish conformity. If you do this, you will reach a state of confusion. Instead, let God simply tell you, "This is my will for you, but I have something better".

Additionally, don't always fall for your friends soothing words. They may make you feel good, but that feeling will soon dissipate, leaving you pondering their words. Jesus in Gethsemane was going to depend on his friends and have them comfort him. They tried their best, but their best was nothing compared to God's knowing will. It's good to be aware that if there was a way for you to fix your own pain, you would not need God. If your friends could fix your pain, you would not need God. If your families could fix your pain, you would not need God. The only one who knows that God can fix your pain, is God. He knows what He has planned for you, and you must come into total alignment with His will to fulfil your purpose.

If you're on the same platform as God, accept things and let go, you will see a new thing burst out from your Spirit; life as the new you. The days of pain will suddenly transform to the days of power.

In this place of conformity, there is no one else. There cannot and should not be anyone but you with your pain, your bleeding, your agony and God. It's a place of intimacy you share with God only. A place where you cannot hang on to friends and seek human comfort. In the place of your press, no friend has what it takes to comfort you, except your heavenly Father.

The place of conformity is a place of prayer. It is a place you close the doors to doubt or distraction. It is a place where you place your pain on the altar, "Your Gethsemane". Luke described Gethsemane as the place of prayer, where Jesus conformed to the will of the Father … *"And being in agony, He prayed more earnestly. Then His sweat became like great drops of blood falling down to the ground."* … Luke 22:44 NKJV.

This final stage is always the most intense; when your inner turmoil is the most intense.

My friend, Jesus is waiting for you right now. Come to the feet of Jesus and surrender all. *"Come to Me, all you who labour and are heavy laden, and I will give you rest"* Matthew 11:28 NKJV. You were not designed to be perfect, He knows you're frail, He knows your weaknesses, He knows your pain, He's been where you've been or where you are ... *"Let us therefore come boldly to the throne of grace, that we may obtain mercy and find grace to help in time of need"* Hebrews 4:16 NKJV. His arms are always open, ready to embrace you. Enter a state of rest by conforming to His will today, and pain will no longer have a hold on your life.

The place of conformity is the place where the perfect will of God is revealed with perfect love.

Chapter Nine
The Love that Never Fails

For we do not have a high priest who is unable to empathise with our weaknesses, but we have one who has been tempted in every way, just as we are — yet he did not sin ... Hebrew 4:15

Human limitations can easily be overlooked or undermined as we focus on the strength God has given unto mankind. What we can do, what we can achieve and what the human race has accomplished, may sometimes make it seem as though we have the power to do all things.

Placing people in a position where they need to function outside of their means to meet our expectations can truly lead to more pain. The agony of disappointment is in its top form when we are exposed to failure, which is to be expected when one's capacity is over estimated. I will say it again, "You cannot give what you don't have". We recognise this limitation for ourselves only. We must consider it an equally high possibility when others are subjected to immense pressure in order to meet our expectations.

The only invincible character and unassailable being is God.

You may not believe in God, and I sincerely do not fault your judgment by any means. I guess we all see things differently at one point or another in our lives. I had the same line of thought, "There is no God," at one point in my life. But let me say this, if you've ever stumbled onto something, for no obvious reason, that is God! ...

His understanding is beyond measure. His sense of perception spans beyond the human scope and horizon, beyond human imagination. His ability to see the future surpasses all human sight. We have a God who is able to give abundantly, beyond what we could ever imagine. His power is beyond measure. His hands created all things, and without Him, nothing would exist. He is the creator of all things, created for His pleasure. Whatever He thinks of, it materialises. He cannot experience failure, and therefore no failure can be found in Him ... He may not be predictable, but He is certainly dependable. He can be trusted to do as He says. No circumstance will alter His plans. His plans are perfect. Relying on this God is the greatest thing we can do to ensure we have the best.

On many occasions, I have placed myself in the peril of disappointment, because I trusted the love of man, as though it was equivalent to the love of God. I have, on several other occasions, placed people on platforms well beyond their means. I found myself in Gethsemane, where my intention was to go to God. My desire to hold onto people, and my trust that they'd always be there for me, almost became a barrier in my quest for victory. Like Jesus, when I realised that everyone around me couldn't feel my pain, I turned to the loving God, who had the power to feel my pain.

That brings me to the story of what I thought was my worst time on earth. It turned out to be one of the greatest success stories of my life.

Those who know my husband well would have heard him speak passionately about his moral failures in the past, specifically regarding sexual immorality. He is not proud of it, but he is obviously grateful to God for setting him free.

When I met this charming man, my husband, Victor, he was everything to me. He is still my world today. I was unaware that I'd just met a man who was dealing with the demon of promiscuity, in his words. He loved the Lord, he was fully anointed, but the stronghold of sexual immorality hung over him.

Months after our marriage, I went to see him in Los Angeles, where he'd been living before we got married. He had stayed in the US for a while, I stayed in the UK. I was so happy and excited at the prospect of spending some time with my husband again.

Sometimes, when God wants to get you out of something, He takes you deeper into it first. The morning after my arrival, my husband had to go to work. Of course, I had to stay home. After he'd gone, I tidied up the house and sat down to watch television. I turned on the television, but couldn't find anything interesting to watch, so I went on his computer, wanting to watch African movies online. As I started up the computer, which he'd given me the password to when he was last in London, but had forgotten about, I saw an icon for photos. Something told me to take a look at the photos. My big sister had been in Los Angeles with my husband the previous week for a revival he'd held at his church. I figured my sister's photos would surely be there as she'd told me that photos had been taken. I clicked on the pictures, and lo and behold, my sister's photo was the first to pop up. I loved it and wanted to see more, so I kept clicking — bad move. That was one thing I regretted doing, but thank God I did.

A few photos later, I was heartbroken. They were unbelievably exotic photos of my husband with another woman, someone who had come to the revival the week before from somewhere in Europe. Not only had photos been taken in our house, they had photos of themselves from when they were at the Universal Studio in Hollywood. It's very difficult to put those images into words, the positions they were in in those photos, I cannot begin to even describe here … you can only imagine the pain I was going through at that moment. The man in the photos was my husband, the one who, I believed, loved me beyond measure. The one I'd given my heart to. Yet there he was, in the arms of another woman. If you're a woman, you could perhaps relate to the excruciating pain that had gripped my heart. I felt like an electric current had passed through me. I was shaken. I broke down into tears, I just couldn't believe what I had seen. I must have looked at those photos at least twenty times. Thousands of things went through my mind, and the voices of those who'd advised me against this marriage in the first place, were playing like music in my mind … the words "Ola you are in another mess," kept repeating themselves, over and over.

I picked up the house phone to call him at work, but the landline was setup to receive calls only. Here I was in a country where I knew nobody. I couldn't call anyone, even if I wanted to. It was only later that I realised that somebody was actually there. Someone I wasn't aware of, but someone who was watching and waiting for me to reach out to him so he could help me. That person was the Holy Spirit. When the Holy Spirit saw that I wasn't going to call him … how was I supposed to call him anyway? I didn't know him, we didn't have that kind of relationship. Anyway, he stretched out this hand, laid it on my chest, whispered into my ears and said, "I want you to pick up the same computer and start typing out all your pain, type out exactly how you feel, what you think of your husband, and your disappointment." It was as though someone was controlling me remotely. I began to type, with uncontrollable tears rolling down my cheeks. When the Holy Spirit was ready, he told me to shut the computer. By the time he'd told me to shutdown, I'd been typing for a good five hours. He also told me to shower, dress well, put make up on and go to the kitchen and start making dinner for my husband. Yeah! I know what you are thinking right now … "Are you serious?" I got up, I didn't question the Holy Spirit, and did all that he'd asked me to do. The process of doing all of this brought a level of peace that I just cannot explain. It wouldn't really make sense if I tried.

At 5:30 that afternoon, my husband walked in. I gave him a hug and a kiss, served the dinner, we ate together and, when it was time for bed, we went to bed and I loved him like I'd never done before. The next day, about twenty minutes after he'd left for work, the spirit of betrayal came over me. However, God did not let me drown in that spirit. He had me on the computer again, doing exactly what I did the day before. This pattern continued for six of the seven days I was there. My husband and I had a lot of fun though. We went shopping and did all sorts. I wasn't in any pain, and he didn't notice a thing.

On my last day, after I'd finished typing as per the Holy Spirit's instructions, he said, "I want you to press the delete button," which I did. He then said, "When your husband comes home tonight, after dinner, tell him all that you've seen and how disappointed you are. I also want you to tell him that you have forgiven him." I did exactly what God told me to do. I wasn't exactly sure about what was happening and I didn't know if I had a future with my husband. This man was supposed to be my hope, my new beginning, especially considering my past was riddled with abuse, abuse and more abuse. Meeting him was the best thing that had happened to me. His personality, love and care gave me a sense of security, but his weakness stood in the way of my desires and expectations. I thought he loved me enough to want to keep me in his life, yet all of what I'd seen in the photos had happened. Are you feeling sorry for me yet? Please don't, because if this had not happened, I would not have had the opportunity to know that God's love never fails.

That night, after talking to my husband about the whole thing, I said to him, "Honey, no hard feelings. I've forgiven you just as the Spirit of the Lord told me to do." There was so much peace within me, it made no sense. My husband couldn't believe that I'd gone through all these emotions and yet I had not, not even for a second, made his life hell. In his previous life, it would have been a different story. He was devastated and ashamed. If not for anything, but the fact he got caught. This left me in a position, as you know, of where I wasn't sure whether I'd come to the end with him. However, in my case, I followed the grace of the Holy Spirit, and forgave.

I woke up the next morning to catch my flight to Maryland for my sister's engagement party. He took me to the airport and I told him that I wasn't sure whether I'd be back, but whatever happened from that moment onwards, he should know that I would always love him. I could see his tears, but I still got on that plane. My flying time was six hours. During all that time, I felt God's presence. I felt like he was there, physically putting his arms around me as I cried uncontrollably for those six hours. I felt his love and his peace. I heard him say, "I want you to know that I love you regardless of what you've done and where you've been. I am the only one who can love you unconditionally, with no attachments. You don't have to do anything, just accept me. Men will always fail you, but I will never fail you. Look at the man you made out to be God in your life, see what he's done to you? If you let me in, you won't have to cry over me, just rejoice." He also told me that He was there when I went through everything I went through. He gave me the peace to enjoy the whole week. "You can have it for life if you let me pour my love over you." That was when I realised that it was God who had helped me through the week, that I wasn't insane, not after what I'd seen with my own eyes. I cried even more then and said, "God, I surrender all to you. If you have a better life to offer me, I will follow and love you."

God always has a way of bringing us to the place of His love. I arrived in Maryland, my older sister picked me up and we went straight to a Pastor's wife's house. My sister had promised her that I could help to fix her hair. My sister had no clue about the pain I was carrying, and I wasn't going to tell her. So to the Pastor's wife's house we went. To cut a long story short, after finishing with her hair, the woman said, "You have made me so beautiful, money is not the right thing to give you, but salvation. Let me introduce Jesus to you." I looked at her, wondering what she was talking about. I'm a church girl. I'd been in church since I was a child. I didn't need any of this. But, before I could even say another word, she grabbed my hand and said, "Repeat after me ..." and that was the last thing I heard. The power of the Holy Spirit came upon me and I began to speak in a different language, a language we called "language of the Spirit". I was instantly baptised with the Holy Spirit.

I shared this story so I could remind you that God's love surpasses love from man. His love cannot be comprehended. God heals every wound, and takes away pain. He turns every sorrow to joy. If He did it for me, He would do it for you. He does not distinguish between different persons. This ordeal was the breakthrough I needed for my husband and I to continue. He couldn't have me without having God, and he loved me enough to realise this.

My husband hopped on a plane and came to Maryland that weekend. This was our turning point. He saw me and instantly realised that I had something I didn't have before – I had Christ in me, the hope of glory. That was it. He set my husband free from the spirit of promiscuity. He healed my heart and made our marriage much better than it had been. Our marriage became a platform of God's grace, and my husband is now helping other men overcome this great demon that is destroying the lives of many great men. We now have a family that we can say is a model of grace.

Sometimes it requires exhausting the dependency on men, and exposure to man's vulnerability, for us to be pushed to fall at the feet of mercy, to receive and accept the love of God. This love has always been available to us through Jesus Christ. In times of desperation, we yearn for the love and companionship of people, we thirst for words of comfort and consolation and eventually become weak and exhausted, as none of these things satisfy our heart's desire, nor does it relieve our pain.

Everyone has their own issues and agendas. Some of the people you trust enough to be there for you during this period of failure and separation have had to wait a long time to see you where you are right now. But unlike humans, the divine God already knows you will arrive at the place of painful separation. He has all the plans in place to support you through this phase.

I remember one thing that broke my heart when we were separated from the church that had given us so much joy. It was the speed with which those who were close to my husband at work, distanced themselves from him. His colleagues would come to his office to discuss their personal life and seek his counsel frequently during the years he was at that company. His bible was always on his desk and everyone knew that he would pick up the bible whenever and share words of direction with them. But when he himself fell into troubled times, he became the person who sought someone to talk to and find comfort in — No! They were all too afraid to be considered close associates of Victor's – who was on the verge of being deported from the country because of his faith, or for being a Pastor. But God's love went ahead of him. He returned home, exhausted and drained on a daily basis, as he searched for a solution from every angle. He kept his face as bright as he could when he stood at the pulpit to preach and share the word of God. But he couldn't stop telling me, "Baby – God loves us." He became strong in God's hand as he felt God shower His love on him, even in the face of mockery and gestures of, "I told you so," from many people. There is nothing like the love of God.

Sometimes I wonder how easy it is to believe how a God we can't see is able to see us, Heaven knows us by name. But I continue to learn *more* as I go through every trial of life. I recount the ordeals and the victories – I can only say God loves me, and His love never fails. I have come to believe that His love cannot fail because love is in His nature, not what He does; love is His purpose, not what He proposes; and love is His infinity, not His limit. The love of God never fails because it is deeply rooted in His Nature. *"But God, who is rich in mercy, for his great love wherewith he loved us"* ... Ephesians 2:4.

Unlike humanity, there is no selfishness in divinity. He is all sufficient by nature and all loving in person.

The love upon which relationships are built, from a human perspective, cannot stand the test of time in most cases. The more you cling to God's love, the quicker you can fill the void that separation creates. The emptiness we experience when we are pulled apart from what we love is quickly eliminated by the fullness of joy that overflows in our hearts when God's love floods it. The bleeding stops, the healings quicken and the recovery is supernatural.

God does not deal with us based on what we have or haven't done. When you understand the loving nature of God, you can access the comfort of His touch during times of heart-break and nerve-wracking separations. People will offer many reasons for why you do not deserve to be treated a certain way, but God's love will show you many reasons why the future is better than the present.

I have shared stories of various instances of pain resulting from separations, but what do you say to a mother who has just lost her seventeen-year-old daughter, and all of her dreams and aspirations with that daughter? Well, the most important thing to remember is that God loves you enough to send his own son to the cross for you. You may not have an explanation for it, but God does. He has loved us with everlasting love because of who He is.

The forces of evil have a negative influence on the world we live in. It can destroy us before we even get started, but because of God's love, we are able to stand up and start afresh. It's easier to start afresh when you know that it is in God's nature to give you a new beginning.

A year and a half after we'd left Saudi Arabia, my husband informed me that I'd been invited to preach to some Egyptian women in Cairo. "Preach? In Cairo?" were my words in return. I couldn't imagine what that would feel like until I entered the auditorium, filled with hundreds of women, and a few men. They were all Egyptians. We had been strictly denied permission to preach to Arabs in Saudi Arabia, having to reaffirm frequently that our services and gatherings were only for Christians, just to keep to the rules of the government. Yet, we were still thrown out of Saudi Arabia because of our preaching. Not even two years later, God opened the doors for me to see the new things he had planned for me in my destiny.

Entering that room and seeing these women's faces, I knew that it had been the love of God that had carried me this far. I just could not wait to open my mouth and pour out that love to these women. When I finally opened my mouth, the place erupted with the power of God, because of His nature of love. This unfailing love is what you need when you are going through the pain of separation that no one can understand.

The love of God never fails because it is purpose driven … *"Having made known unto us the mystery of His will, according to His good pleasure which He hath purposed in Himself."* … Ephesians 1:9

God's love is purpose driven. Love is not what He proposes, it is what He intends. Everything that is happening in your life right at this moment, as bad as it may seem, with eyes of the love of God, you can look and find His purpose.

I read the story of Hannah, who was separated from the fruit of the womb for a long time in her marriage. She was tormented by her mate, as the bible rightfully put it, the woman who she shared her man with. The story is one of its kind in the bible. There was no way she would have dedicated her baby unto the Lord, had she not gone through the pain of separation. When she finally had the child, she gave the child unto God, who then became the child of transition. This child then stood in the place of Israel's transition, in its move from the hands of the morally bankrupt priestly family of Eli.

Israel had suffered in the hands of Eli's children. Women were raped, people were conned, and men were made to forcefully serve them. The chosen people of God, Israel, the people God loved with everlasting love, watched as their lives fell under the control of another task master in their own promised land. The pain of Hannah became the power of Israel in purpose. The child, who had been withheld by God for so long before joining her mother, was now the Prophet to the nation. This is a reflection of the purpose-driven love God has for us.

I, not once, saw any love in a God that allowed my husband to labour so hard in building our church and then, suddenly and unexpectedly, having to leave the country without much explanation or room for discussion. But the more I understood what God was doing with us, wherever in the world we were, the more I saw the love of God. Those in Jordan and Egypt were so loved by God, He allowed me to go through that pain for them. Many have since been blessed by my husband's mentoring and support, since his move to the Maghreb.

One day, you will become a blessing to someone with your testimony. After all, God's love, that never fails, has brought you through with victory, to the other side ...

"And to know the love of Christ, which passeth knowledge, that ye might be filled with all the fullness of God." ... Ephesians 3:19

God's love has no boundaries. That is why it cannot be compared to the affections that fade with time and motives. The love of God is not colour blind, where he only shows compassion to a black person, not a white person ... no, His love goes beyond our comprehension. How can the same God you and I offended and sinned against, come to stand in our place in judgment? Limitless love; the love of God is indescribable.

It is this love that sets Peter free from the bondage of guilt that would have tormented him and impeded his purpose.

When I was leaving Saudi Arabia, I was filled with so much resentment and anger towards the country. I just couldn't see how a nation that subdued human rights and undermined the freedom of human beings made by God, had a place on earth. I questioned God, "How could a nation, that was so paranoid of the gospel of Jesus Christ, be allowed to be a nation?" Forget the fact that it was an oil rich country, if not the richest oil country in the world. It didn't add up for me. But, the love of God is limitless. A few days before we left the country, God said, "I love them, I love Saudi Arabia, just like I love every human race. And what have they done?"

When we went to say goodbye to my husband's boss, the Saudi man was filled with such a sense of guilt on behalf of his country, he didn't know what to say to me. But I told him that I would always love his country because God loved it ...

The bone of contention Jonah had with God is based on the love of God for the same people He'd sworn to destroy. Jonah could not comprehend why he had to go through the pain of being separated from his comfort zone, or why he'd been made to leave his pleasant home and go to Nineveh to reach out to the people God had considered sinners.

Jonah could not see past his own pain in order to see the purpose-driven, limitless love of God. This made him both angry and depressed. However, God did not waste any time in showing him how limitless His love was.

When the tension of our inner pain and the intensity of God's love collides, a spark of purpose is produced, which takes us into the realms of unlimited opportunities. Every time we see our problems through the eyes of God's love, we rise up and fly with the wings of His grace.

The things we are attached to, the places we are tied to and the person we have bonds with, are all part of God's plan. But God's love moves like a wave at the right moment. It can pull us away with such force, it leaves nothing but pain. Although, His soothing balm is available to heal us until we are strong enough to embark upon the next assignment of our destiny, where we can prosper in our next level of purpose.

The pain of separation cannot outlive the purpose of God that is rooted in His love for you. I learnt the hard way, but I was blessed the heavenly way.

Friends may fail you, family may fault you, husbands may walk away from you, wives may desert you, but God's love is forever certain.

Yes, I thought you would be there for me; yes, I thought you would understand my position; yes, I thought you would walk with me and stand by me, but you didn't. That was not your fault, it was a divine set up. It all happened so that I would understand that there was another love I needed to cling to more — the love of God.

Do you know why you can't feel my pain? It's because you do not have the power to understand the pain that comes with purpose. I didn't understand it either. I would have fallen into a state of depression, and without the love of God, I would have committed suicide. Had it not been for the love of God, I would have given up on my dreams and let people's action alter the course of my life in the wrong direction. It was the love of God that sustained me. This same love is available to you. Regardless of what you are going through and how much humiliation this separation has caused you, one thing is for sure, God's love surpasses your loss. "Many are the afflictions of the righteous", a common bible quote. Many people want the righteous part but not the affliction. It all works together for our good when we understand God's love. When you recognise that God has experienced where you are now, it won't matter if people can't feel your pain.

"If God can feel your pain, He can fill your heart!"

Chapter Ten

Putting it Together Again …

The Lord said, "Simon, Simon, behold, Satan asked to have you, that he might sift you as wheat, but I prayed for you, that your faith wouldn't fail. You, when once you have turned again, establish your brothers" … Luke 22:31-32

A key factor that aids the shattering of your destiny is the long lasting discouragement that stops you from seeing past your loss. There is no doubt that we heal from the bleeding and wound of separation. It is whether we go beyond the scar that is important and most crucial. It is one thing for you to be bruised, cut deep and crushed; it is another to heal deep enough to be ready to invest again.

In place of displacement, replacement doesn't come fast enough. Jesus was the only man who had ever vowed to reconstruct a temple, one that had taken years to build, in three days. No man can ever walk in his shoes. I think this is the reason why, after losing a large part of what we'd built with a lot of effort to separation, the fear of going back to pursue our purpose was always evident and potentially obstructive.

What I would like to do at this point, is let you know that there isn't an option to quit. I want to reveal why it is not God's will for you to give up on your dreams. I will also take a little time to let you know how, after you have healed, you must reap the rewards. With my limited experience, I would like to help you with the why.

It takes being separated from your passion to initiate your pain. It should take all of hell to stop you from going back to your passion, no matter how many times you lose.

The persons, the places or the things you've lost are just the output of your dreams and passion. You have certainly not lost your dreams.

Your spouse may have left, but your dream of a perfect marriage and being a happy wife or husband remains. Of course, I understand you lost the job you considered your dream job, but you haven't lost your dream to reach the top in your career, in the company of your choice. In the case of my husband and I, it was the loss of the church in Saudi Arabia. I was certain that our passion and dream to build the best church in a Muslim nation was never lost. We should never let the scars scare our dreams. The lost should not stop the love.

Jesus was on his way out, but he knew the crucial role Peter would play in the future of the church. He also knew that the devil would do anything to separate Peter from that purpose and destiny.

Therefore, Jesus intended to do everything he could to ensure Peter knew, and was fully aware, that he could not give up on his dream. This is how I know that God does not take pleasure from our quitting, only in our winning. God's love will take you back to the right place, the right person or the right thing. Whatever you've been through, avoid letting the scar deter you from seeing the place, the person, or the thing you need to see. Scars instil a sense of mistrust and doubt. You become suspicious of everyone and everything. You become overly cautious and risk averse. This happens when you are healed from the pain of separation, but continue to focus on the scar. How hard would it be for Peter to hold his head up and step into the position of leadership when he was faced with people who had seen him fail miserably where he was expected to succeed. It wouldn't be easy, I presumed, but Jesus had made it clear that Peter must move past the scars and step back into his dream again. The song writer of "Dance Again" by Life church Bradford in UK, wrote: *tears will dry, your heart will mend, scars will heal and you will dance again.*

I was involved in a car accident in 1987. My mother had died and I was on my way to the funeral when this incident happened. The car was a right-off, so was I. After two hours in the hospital, the doctors told my brother, who'd been driving the car, "Sorry Mr Collins, we did all we could, but she didn't make it." What happened next is not something you would believe. The accident had happened in West Africa, where there aren't enough morgues to hold the deceased. A corpse had to be removed before another could take its place in the morgue. This was the case with me. I was declared dead at about nine in the morning, left on the stretcher, waiting for an available morgue to take me in. At about nine thirty at night, one became available. They started preparing my body for the morgue. In those twelve hours, my other brother and uncle, who had joined my brother at the hospital, had become strong believers in the God of the Universe. They'd spent the last twelve hours believing and praying, pleading to God for my return. Exactly thirteen hours after the doctor's proclamation, God brought me back to life. I became a living being, a testimony to the unbelievers in that hospital. He did it in the ancient days, and He is still very much around to do it again.

The accident was so bad that there wasn't a single place in my body that hadn't been affected. My head was hurt so badly, you could see my skull. My right knee had to be stitched together before I could move it. I almost lost my right eye, and my shoulders had to be stitched. My whole body was totally messed up by this accident. This left a lot of scars on my body. I was in and out of the hospital for six months. My head was bandaged for nine months. All my wounds eventually healed, but the scars are still there, especially on one side of my head, where the hair doesn't grow any more. I'd always dreamt of growing up and becoming a lady driving a car. It has always been my passion. This accident shattered that dream, sent it from my consciousness completely. I became so paranoid about getting in a car, I couldn't even contemplate driving. But I rekindled that passion and did not let this accident destroy my dream. Every time I look at my scars, I ask myself, "How did I survive that accident? How did I overcome the pain? How did I move past the fear of being in a car again to driving a car after all that had happened?" Then I came to the conclusion that it was the power and the love of God that helped made me reach beyond my pain and my scars.

Firstly, God made sure I believed and understood that it was not His intention for me to be left with deformations following this accident. His desire was for me to not hold onto my scars instead, to overcome my fears and sit behind the wheels. His power helped me see beyond my scars. It was His love that set me free from the claws of the enemy, where I would have lived in fear. Though the accident had left physical scars all over my body, my deepest, emotional scar was that I hadn't been able to attend my mother's funeral. I wrote earlier, in chapter seven, about how I'd missed my mother's last breath by two hours. I had been looking forward to paying my last respects to her at her funeral; I was deprived of this by the enemy. This is the deepest scar in my heart. It cannot be seen, touched, bandaged, nor medicated. It is a scar that will be there forever. So how do I deal with a scar that will determine how I live my life from that point onwards?

I know the pain of your divorce has healed, but it has left you with a scar. You had always dreamt of that beautiful marriage, but it didn't happen. The relationship you thought would last all eternity, has failed. Firstly, you must recognise that God wants you to recover from your loss. He wants you to keep moving forward. He didn't create you to be beaten and hidden from existence. He doesn't want you to put your life on hold because of a failed marriage. He doesn't want you to give up on your dreams of being a wife and maybe a mother, a husband and a father. I know your scar reminds you of what someone has done to you; or each time you look at your children, you're reminded of what you created together. Thinking too much about your sorrows will drown you in depression. I want to encourage you to close the door on your scars and open your eyes to the greater things God has planned for you. You cannot let your scars stop you from loving again. You cannot allow your scars to keep you from trusting again. You cannot let your scars prevent your future happiness. Your tears will dry, your heart will mend, your scars will heal and you will be happy again, if only you don't quit. I once heard someone say that it's not about the number of times you are knocked down, it's about your ability to bounce back. It is not over until you win.

This reminds me of the story of David in 2 Samuel 30. David had gone to fight a war. When he returned, he realised that the Amalekites had invaded the South and Ziklag, where he had left his wives and children. The whole city had been set on fire and the Amalekites had taken women and children away, including David's wives and children. David and others who were with him, raised their voices and wept until they had no more tears left to shed (I Samuel 30:4 NKJV).

David faced a serious crisis in his leadership. He was greatly distressed, not only because of his personal grief, but from the difficult situation he now faced. The people had spoken of stoning him. He was being blamed for what the Amalekites had done to their wives and their children. The people believed that, had they not gone to war with him, they would have been around to protect their families.

David was under a lot of pressure. He grieved heavily, and probably regretted going to war without ensuring his family, and that of the other soldiers, were well protected. He had many "if onlys" going through his mind. Things he should have done differently. His failure was not having done his homework properly, leaving the door open to the enemy, allowing them to captivate the families and destroy the city with a strength that was strong enough to beat him down. It could have crippled him as a leader. It could have left him feeling like a failure. The scar the enemy had left behind could have prevented him from ever trying again. But not David. He knew exactly who he was. He knew he'd been created for a purpose. He knew he had a destiny to fulfil, and he wasn't going to let anything the enemy did prevent him from fulfilling his purpose, his dreams and visions of becoming King of Israel one day, so he shook it off. He shut down every avenue of depression, every door of fear, doubt, and anything else that could potentially throw him off the course of his purpose.

This is what the enemy hopes you will do. He wants you to drown in your pain and make your scars the steps that bring you down from your mountain top to the pit created by the enemy. You must not let them bring you down. You must shake off all the scars, the disappointment, the guilt, and the failure, and do exactly what David did.

The bible said "*But David strengthened himself in the LORD his God*". Unlike most of us who, when we go through difficult times, turn to people who cannot understand our pain, nor heal it. David knew where to turn when he was facing a time of crisis. He had learnt to wait on God and was confident of God's eventual deliverance. As shown in his writing in the book of Psalm: *I waited patiently for the LORD; And He inclined to me, and heard my cry. He also brought me up out of a horrible pit, Out of the miry clay, And set my feet upon a rock, And established my steps ...* Psalms 40:1-2 NKJV.

He turned to the only God that had the power to heal and restore. David didn't go around thinking about his loss, though he was in pain. He did not allow his pain, however, keep him down. Nor did he let his pain crowd his thoughts of what to do next. He wasn't going to give up on his dreams of becoming a leader, a husband and a father. His pain was not strong enough to keep him away from his purpose and his destiny. *So David inquired of the LORD, saying, "Shall I pursue this troop? Shall I overtake them?" And He answered him, "Pursue, for you shall surely overtake them and without fail recover all." ...* I Samuel 30:8 NKJV

Today, the Lord is saying to you: if you do not give up, if you do not give in, if you do not quit your dreams, you will recover. You will not recover some things, but all things. So David went after the Amalekites and the story went: *So David recovered all that the Amalekites had carried away, and David rescued his two wives. And nothing of theirs was lacking, either small or great, sons or daughters, spoil or anything which they had taken from them; David recovered all ...* I Samuel 30:18-19 NKJV.

The deep scars left from our pain can put us in a place where the world around us starts to make no sense. A world where there are no hopes and wishes. Some people never recover from it. Not because they don't want to, they just don't know how to. Their pain overpowers their dreams. Their scars prevent their achievements. If you are the person I have just described, you need to know that there is a purpose behind why you were created. You need to understand and believe that you were not created to waste away, you were created to fulfil your purpose and your destiny.

Your assignment is to be able to soar above all circumstances and situations. The good book tells us that we will account to Him, no matter how we live the life He has given us.

Your God given assignment, or call it a command if you wish, is to be fruitful, to multiply, to fill the earth and subdue it. "*Then God blessed them and said Be fruitful and multiply; fill the earth and subdue it; have dominion over the fish of the sea, over the birds of the air, and over every living thing that moves on the earth*" (Genesis 1:28

NKJV). You are to have dominion over all that God has created.

To be fruitful means to be productive or conducive, or producing in abundance. Anyone who does not look past their scars, cannot be productive. If you cannot let go of your pain, you will continue to see your scars every time the opportunity to be happy comes your way. You will not be productive and you will actually stagnate, like a monument that stays in one place, not moving and not to be moved.

To multiply means you must grow. If you want to grow, you cannot live in your past, cannot let the past hold you down or dictate your present and your future. Your life of growing is like opening a bank account, depositing money regularly, and letting your money grow. If you leave your account empty, it won't grow. There will come a point where the bank will close down the account because it is not functional.

The difference between God and your bank account is that He will never shut you down. As a matter of fact, God specialises in opening bigger accounts in our heavenly bank, one that is incomparable to our world's banks. The heavenly bank, where you needn't deposit money for your account to grow. No one can beat that. His love and grace is the activation code to your account.

One of the things I've seen God do in my life, and in the lives of many others I've spoken to, is that He publicises your "comeback" in a big way. So when people see you, they instantly know that you've been withdrawing from an account that never runs dry. I call it "restoration".

"So I will restore to you the years that the swarming locust has eaten, The crawling locust, The consuming locust, And the chewing locust ... You shall eat in plenty and be satisfied, And praise the name of the LORD your God, Who has dealt wondrously with you; And My people shall never be put to shame." Joel 2:25-26 NKJV. This is a promise to those who are willing to look past their scars. It is a promise to those who are willing to try again, to be happy, to restore their life back to how it was before the enemy attacked. It's a promise to those who are determined to look at their scars and say, "You will no longer have power over me. I'm coming out, I'm setting myself free from my pain, my past, my failures, my wounds and my scars." It is for those who are tired of sitting in the pit of depression or suicide. If you fall into one of these categories, I congratulate you on your return party. Heaven is celebrating you right now, the devil and his team are crying as they have lost the battle over you again.

As a child of God, you were commanded to subdue. To subdue means you have "authority" over your pain. You have been given the power to stand strong in the face of adversity. Your previous pain and scars are under your control. You are ahead of your enemy's wiles. Being in charge means you are the dictator. It means you have the authority and capacity to tell people what to do, how to do it and when to do it. If President Obama ordered his Chief of Armed Forces to bring his soldiers together and go to war today, the chief of staff would have no right to comment or decline the authority of the President of the United States. Chances are, if he did, he would lose his job and the benefits that come with it. That is why, when you listen to people's experiences and hear what they've been through, as a Christian, you begin to ask yourself, "How did they make it?" They made it because they understood the "authority" given to them from the foundation of the world. They are capable of being in control of everything and anything that comes their way. They not only understand it, as understanding it is one thing, but they know how and when to apply it.

When we talk about understanding and the use of our authority, the story of the prodigal son always come to my mind.

"But when he came to himself, he said, 'How many of my father's hired servants have bread enough and to spare, and I perish with hunger! I will arise and go to my father, and will say to him, Father, I have sinned against heaven and before you, and I am

no longer worthy to be called your son. Make me like one of your hired servants'" … Luke 15:17-19 NKJV.

The prodigal son was able to pull himself together because he knew whose son he was, and the right he had lost as a son. If you read carefully, it's apparent that he did not allow for his own mistakes to bring him down. He knew that his place was not with the lower class. He knew the benefits enjoyed by his father's servants. As he was the son, this placed him in a higher place of authority. He didn't let the shame of what he'd done to his family hold him back from taking his rightful position. He'd rather go back to his father's house and be a servant there than stay on the streets eating thrown-away food. That's a clear message to those who thought they could never go back to where they used to be, let alone the higher positions they once held. This is to remind you of the "authority" that has been placed in your hands, and to encourage you that "now is the time to use that authority". Set yourself free, go back to your father's house. His arms will always be open to welcome you back. He loves you and he wants to see you happy again.

Talking about dominion refers to the right that has been reserved exclusively for you by God. It basically means that you are to take your rightful position. You didn't work for this right, didn't pay anything for it, nor did you do anything to deserve this right. It was given to you freely; a territory that has been assigned to you, and you alone. Anyone who comes into your territory, without your permission, is trespassing. God wants you to know that whatever you choose to do in your territory, it is your business, no one has the right to question you, or fault you.

It is also important for you to be aware that you do not have to allow pain to settle with you in your territory. You don't have to allow your past failures to reside in your present territory. You need not allow guilt to reside there either. Scars do not have the right to "Stay with you forever" if you do not allow such dominance over your life. Taking control of your own destiny is the key to freeing yourself from anything that will hold you back from a new beginning.

Allow me to walk you through the three pitfalls you must avoid when you have reached the peak of the pain of separation, when you want to get your life back again: FEAR, MISTRUST and DOUBT form the points of a triangle that has the potential to distract you from your destiny.

Fear is an unpleasant emotion. It is generally triggered by the threat of danger, pain, or harm. It places us in uneasy circumstances. Fear often creeps in when we try something and are unsuccessful.

Fear will also remind you of your failures, your guilt, and your past pain. Although, it will not stop there. Fear will make you believe there is no reason for you to move on with your life. It manifests itself in your face every time you try to put your pain behind you, and it will seem as though you can't afford to invest in what you had done before your attempt failed.

Let's take someone who lost their million-dollar business to a fire. Fear could or would stop this person from ever wanting to invest in another business. Every time business opportunities arose, fear would make this person wonder whether the incident would happen again. It is similarly applicable to a failed job, or failed marriage. Fear is the giant that stands between you, your pain and your future. If you don't eliminate it from your mind, it has the potential to mess up your entire life. You will not be able to lead a fulfilling life. You will not be able to multiply and grow in every aspect of your life.

God promised the Israelites the land of Canaan, as an inheritance from the time of Abraham. When it was the time for them to inherit the land, Moses sent some men into the land of Canaan to see it and report back to him. They saw how great the land was, how it really did flow with milk and honey, just how God had described the land to them. Despite the greatness and potential they saw in the land, the numbers of inhabitants there overwhelmed them.

Their fear overshadowed the promises the land offered. I believe they were still living with the fear of their experiences from when they had to leave Egypt. They saw giants. The giants were their fear. It crippled their minds and their belief in all God had done for them since leaving Egypt.

This is what fear does to you if you allow it to take hold. It will make you trade your future for your past. You cannot let this happen. God has planned a great future for you. One that is full of joy, promotion, abundance, wealth, health and all that your heart desires. Your "motto" should be, "I am an overcomer, and I will overcome my every fear. I will not settle for less than what my God has in store for me." Let, "I will possess my possession" be your daily confession, and work on it until you have seen your enemy (fear) cave under your feet. Bringing it all back together will defile the fear. It may be difficult, it may come with a struggle, and you may have to do some crazy things. Nevertheless, remember, no one says, "comeback" is a bed of roses. If you can hold onto your dreams and vision and not give up, it is achievable. So go ahead, Champion, go ahead, defile your fears, and get your life back again. Aim to make it even better than it was before. God is on your side.

Mistrust is the concept of not trusting others because of your past experiences with other people. It arises when you've lost your confidence in people, things or places. You are sceptical and suspicious about everything, everyone and every place. It is not your fault that you feel you can't trust anymore. Trust is fragile and easily broken, something that is hard to do. This is mainly because of what you've been through. I understand that your last relationship failed because he cheated on you. I understand the molestation you suffered at the hands of your abuser. I understand that you were lied to, leaving you not wanting to trust again. I feel your pain. I've also been through a lot myself, from rejection to rape, to being abused, lied to and cheated on, countless times. I've even been beaten by a man for things that made no sense to me. These things happened simply because I allowed certain people into my life. Believe me, I know about the pain and the scars left within your heart. I also know that you don't want to be where you are right now. I know you want to be free of the pain and suffering. You wish to be able to trust again. I know that deep down, you cherish happiness, you want to love again, you want to be loved again, but you just don't have the will power to do so right now. You also want to trust, but aren't sure who to trust.

To be able to trust again, the first step is to put all your trust in God, so He can guide your thoughts. You must believe that if He has strengthened and brought you this far, He will see you through it all and will not quit until He sees you back on your feet again.

Secondly, you must understand that God knows more than you know, and that He is able to send the right people to you. He will not allow your foot to be moved from where it is strongly grounded.

He who keeps you will not slumber. Behold, He who keeps Israel Shall neither slumber nor sleep. The LORD is your keeper ... Psalms 121:3 NKJV.

Thirdly, you must understand that people are different. The relationship you have with people will naturally vary. The environment or the surroundings will also vary. Just like yesterday was different to today. Likewise, everything you do or go through will change. God made sure that when He created Adam and Eve, He did not create them to be similar. He made one out of dust and the other out of a finished product of dust. This is why I can confidently tell you that you will not always be where you are. Note what happens from the moment a baby is born, to the day it dies. You will see daily changes in the child's growth. Similarly, your fingers, if you observe carefully, are also changing.

In the bible, there is a story of a woman who refused to let her past relationships hold her back from trying over, and over, and over again. It is the story of the Samaritan woman in the Gospel of John, chapter four. She came to draw water from a well and met Jesus there. Jesus started a conversation with her. If I was to use today's terminology, I would say that Jesus was chatting her up. He was telling her some seemingly impossible things. The woman looked at Jesus and said, "It's unbelievable that you're talking to me, but to ask me for water sounds even worse. You are a Jew and I am a Samaritan, we are not supposed to be talking." I like the story because the Samaritan woman had overcome all past abuses, pain, failures, and fear. By putting her past behind her, she was not afraid to talk to men.

The other thing I like about the Samaritan woman's story is not the fact that she was on her sixth marriage when Jesus met her, it was her ability to keep trying until she found her happiness. She was determined to love, and be loved. She refused to let her past, or the scars that other men had left in her, keep her away from her dreams of being a wife. I believe she would have faced a lot of shame, disgrace, humiliation, and gossip within her community, due to the culture back then. But she didn't let her community, the gossip, or shame overpower her dreams. She cared little about what others said. I sincerely think that that's what Jesus was attracted to when he passed through her village. Jesus had no real reason to pass through Samaria. His only reason was her. What she wanted from a man was love and care, acceptance and security. Even when she didn't find this, she persevered and eventually met Jesus, who gave her soul the rest it needed. He gave her a new life.

If you want to live your life to the full, you have to embrace the spirit of the Samaritan woman. This is achievable by simply not letting your past determine or define your future. You must fight the voices in your head that tell you not to trust anyone. The thing is, you cannot live life without people. First of all, it would be a miserable life. Secondly, you'd be robing yourself of the joy that is sure to come. A joy you will never experience if you have difficulty trusting again. Child of God, you have been equipped, empowered, and strengthened. The bible states that you must renew your mind daily, "Arise and shine for your light has come, and the glory of the Lord has risen upon you". Believe in the Lord, your God, and believe in yourself too. Kick the devil in the face, step out and step up.

Doubt is one of the pitfalls on the path to recovery. It stems from a lack of confidence. It is the state of being unsure about what's next. It's the feeling of uncertainty or lack of conviction. Simply put, it is the "lack of faith in someone or in something". Doubting other people is one thing, doubting yourself is worse.

Our past failures effortlessly cast a shadow of doubt on us as soon as we enter a similar territory.

It is a form of a risk alert that is set to trigger when a process operates outside of the set parameters. It is a warning alarm that goes off when danger is imminent.

However, it is God trying to return something you lost, but in a better shape or perfected form. It's likely for you to swiftly reject it because it feels, looks and sounds like the path of agony you experienced before. "I don't want to go through that again, not after all I went through last time." That seems to be the catch phrase of a defeated mind. You doubt people, you doubt yourself, and in the process, you allow the new, and possibly best opportunities, pass you by.

After all we'd been through in Saudi Arabia, and the subsequent pain and betrayal I'd experienced, bringing people together to start another church, effectively submitting myself to the work of the Ministries, was the last thing on my mind. I remembered my husband telling me about a building he'd seen in Cairo. To him, it seemed like the building was already prepared for him to form a church. I was completely sick to my stomach. He went on and on, telling me about the layout and structure of the building, the location and how he could imagine people arriving on buses, and how he felt he could create a great church in that city. I couldn't understand what was going through his mind. We'd just left Saudi Arabia, having been treated like criminals for pushing for the freedom for Christians to worship without fear, and here was this husband of mine, still thinking the same thing in a country that was not very different to Saudi Arabia. Deep inside me, I had a passion for the work of the Ministries. It's often the things we do best that brings us happiness as a family. I know that this was one thing my husband did not stress about, and I knew this was my passion. But note how quickly our passion can be dampened by the pain of the past. "God definitely didn't take us through the pain of separation to leave us in a vacuum," was a conclusion my husband often came to. I'm not saying that we should be oblivious of the fact that there are bad people in the world, that things will not always go the way we want it to, but that we must not let that hold us back from following our passion, rising above the doubt that can be overwhelming.

"This same Jesus, Who is taken up from you into heaven, shall so come in like manner as ye have seen Him go into heaven." ... Acts 1:11

On numerous occasions, I have thought about the content of this book as my anchor point. Pretty much every time I was on the verge of giving up on my dreams. Recently, the tables turned. My husband started doubting the influential family who were working tirelessly to ensure my husband could return to Saudi Arabia to pursue the dream of building the Centre for Christianity there. He was too consumed with doubt and mistrust, and I had to be the one to bring him back to our faith and energy, urging him not to give up on what God had laid on his heart as a vision. This book was my way of preaching to my husband.

Look at Jesus, who arrived with the passion to save the world. Look at the magnitude of his suffering and the agony of betrayal. Think of all the evil that was spoken against him, and how the world he'd come to save had yet to accept him. But, is he coming back again? That sounds too difficult to believe. But it is true. God is in the process of creating a "comeback". He will take pleasure in the opportunity to do it all over again. God himself has done similar things several times, why would you not be able to stand up to your purpose, no matter the failures of the past.

The devil is doing everything to stop Jesus from coming back. He has even placed doubt in the minds of many, who are now asking, "When is he going to return?" or "Is he really going to come back?"

This is possibly similar to the doubts in your mind right now. I have been through it myself. People are likely to ask you the same questions, casting doubt on your own dreams: "Are you going to get married again after losing the man or the woman you considered the love of your life?" "Would you ever Pastor again after losing the church you built with such passion?" I think your answer should be affirmative. I think you must be ready to say, "No matter how long it takes, I will not give up on my dreams." I think you should be able to let your critics know that you are on your way back up.

Life may throw a roadblock, but God has a building block to overcome this. God has everything we need to rise above our doubts. People, places and things are in place to help you do better. This was our belief when my husband and I stepped into new waters to participate in the race of our dreams and destiny, with passion and faith. We didn't have all the resources we needed to fulfil our own desires, but we had the passion to see the future, which allowed us to take things one step at a time. We don't have the people we need to rebuild, but we are blessed with people who will help us through the initial phase. We don't have the right skills to express what we would like to bring to the journey of recreating it, but we are equipped with what it takes to push to the point where we will need help. And God will send help. I just know that God will help us. But you must be determined to get back up, and put it all back together again ... God is able!

In a Nutshell

Separation is one of life's phenomena. It is inevitable. We will have to deal with it at one point or another during the course of our lives. The pain that comes with it can make or break you. Choose to make the best of it. I came to the following conclusions after surviving a life time of pain caused by separation:

- There is time for everything. Separation makes that statement come true. It is important to accept it as a time bound event that will occur when the time comes.

- Life is a journey to your destiny. The in-betweens are merely temporary destinations, and should not be considered the end of your journey. Something bigger is waiting for you in your next move, but only if you don't let separation hold you back.

- The investment you put into a relationship is the root cause of the pain, but the harvest will be waiting for you. There is no doubt that God can see your tears and feel your pain.

- Holding people responsible for the separation, or taking offence from the way people treat you during the course of separation, is not conducive to your healing. Always remember that people can only give what they have. Most people you rely on, do not have the capacity to join you as you journey to your next level. It may not be intentional when they leave you. They just don't have a role to play in this next phase. Free your mind of what you consider offensive and prepare for a new adventure.

- The feeling of guilt that arises when you think you should have been there for someone, a friend, family member, or even your church, when they were facing troubled times, is normal amongst people. Do not hold yourself overly accountable for what God is in control of. It was probably not your fault, rather it was the will of God that prevailed. Do your best and leave the rest to God.

- Be ready to confront your fears. Accept the fear that naturally accompanies instances where you are dealing with something larger than yourself. Shed the tears, speak your pain and let it loose. At the end, submit to the will of God. Let this phrase, "Thy will be done," carry you on. No matter what the situation is, God's will is perfect.

- Reaching full acceptance of God's love for me went a long way to giving me the strength to escape the pit of depression. He loves me, but I cannot say why. God's love is far more than you can imagine. He will never leave you in a state of perdition. He has your life planned out, framed with love.

- Stand up to your new challenge. Do not let this pain of separation stop you. Rekindle your passion for your purpose. Reaffirm to yourself, over and over again, that your dream will stay alive, despite the pain you endured in the past.

57712605R00131

Made in the USA
Charleston, SC
23 June 2016